BUSINESS BUILDERS

HOW TO BECOME AN ADMIRED & TRUSTED CORPORATE LEADER

DAN ADAMS

Business Builders: How to Become an Admired and Trusted Corporate Leader, Copyright © 2023 by Dan Adams

Published by The AIM Institute
2206 20th Street
Cuyahoga Falls, OH 44223

ISBN 9798854426183

Contact the author or publisher at www.TalkWithAIM.com.

All rights reserved. Except as permitted under U.S. Copyright Act of 1976, no part of this publication may be reproduced, distributed, or transmitted in any form or by any means, or stored in a database or retrieval system, without the prior written permission of the publisher.

DO YOU THINK LIKE A BUSINESS BUILDER?

To find out, take this free, five-minute assessment at

www.AreYouABusinessBuilder.com.

Download your confidential, personalized report showing your Business Builder Score (max 100) and see how your thinking aligns with twenty Business Builder Beliefs.

For each Business Builder Belief, you'll see a brief explanation that includes page references from this book for further exploration.

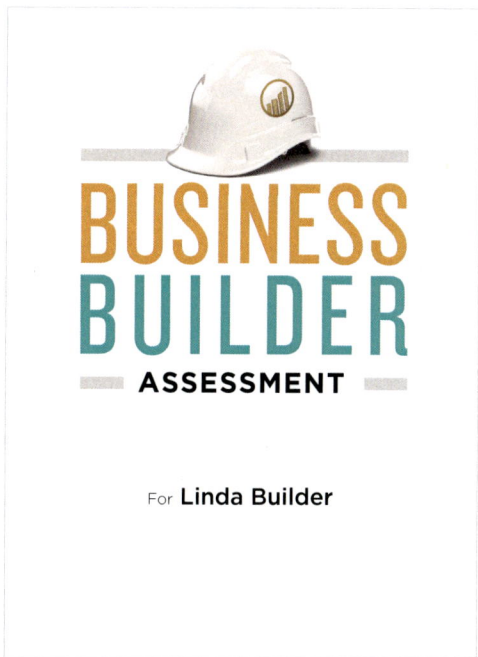

CONTENTS

Ch. 1: **Builders and Climbers** — 1

Ch. 2: **What Is a Business Builder?** — 11

Ch. 3: **Builders Embrace Their First Duty** — 23

Ch. 4: **Builders Avoid False Goals** — 35

Ch. 5: **Builders Drive Profitable, Sustainable Growth** — 43

Ch. 6: **Builders Pursue Market-Facing Innovation** — 53

Ch. 7: **Builders Have Long Time Horizons** — 71

Ch. 8: **Builders Know Finance Is a Spectator Sport** — 85

Ch. 9: **Builders Strengthen Business Capabilities** — 97

Ch. 10: **Builders Understand Customer Needs** — 109

Ch. 11: **Does This Apply to Our Business?** — 127

Ch. 12: **How Do We Change Our Business?** — 139

Ch. 13: **How Do I Become a Builder?** — 147

Appendix A: **The Special Advantages of B2B** — 159

Appendix B: **How to Understand B2B Customer Needs** — 173

Acknowledgments — 193

About the Author — 195

About AIM Institute — 196

Endnotes — 198

CHAPTER 1

BUILDERS AND CLIMBERS

> "On this team, we're all united in a common goal . . . to keep my job."
>
> —LOU HOLTZ

CHAPTER 1: **BUILDERS AND CLIMBERS**

Are you a Builder or a Climber? Either approach could get you to the top of a company, but the journeys are quite different.

Meet Cal and Bill. Cal is a Climber and CEO of a billion-dollar company. He's sharp, hardworking, and has always been good at "managing up." His unspoken creed? *Whatever interests my boss fascinates me.*

Cal is also a wizard at understanding financial reports and "unlocking value" in businesses. For Cal this has meant taking over well-run divisions and cutting costs for long-term efforts like exploratory research and pursuing adjacent markets. By the time these actions damaged each business's future, Cal had moved on to run another business.

Bill is a Builder and also the CEO of a billion-dollar company. He got his hands dirty early in his career by working in operations and learning what made his business tick. He found his true passion while working on new product teams.

For Bill, nothing matched the satisfaction of learning what customers truly wanted, delivering meaningful innovation, and watching the sales roll in.

CAL THE CLIMBER

- Knows financial reports
- Near time horizon
- Inside-out perspective
- Denominator focus
- Results reporter

BILL THE BUILDER

- Knows new products
- Far time horizon
- Outside-in perspective
- Numerator focus
- Results creator

Cal is a near time horizon guy, thinking in months or quarters. If financial results were published every fortnight, his time horizon would be fortnights. Cal wants to look good whenever someone is looking. Bill is a far time horizon guy. He thinks in years because that's what it takes for new products to deliver needle-moving revenue and for employee training to deliver serious change.

Cal thinks inside-out, focusing first on internal financial results. Bill thinks outside-in, meeting the needs of customers—which ultimately is the only way to improve those financial results. Funny thing, but early in their careers they each had company phone systems that rang once for incoming internal calls and twice for external calls from customers. Cal always made sure he picked up the single rings, and Bill never missed the double rings.

Cal focuses on the denominator and Bill on the numerator. Cal's first question for improving ROI is, *What costs can we cut?* Bill asks, *How can we grow this business?* Cal's in trouble if his predecessor was also a Climber.

CAL'S IN TROUBLE IF HIS PREDECESSOR WAS ALSO A CLIMBER.

Denominator work eventually reaches a point of diminishing returns, with nothing left to cut. Bill can always find meaningful work since revenue growth has no upper limit.

Cal is a results reporter; Bill is a results *creator*. When financial results are reported, they reflect the quality and quantity of products created *years* earlier. Cal can explain these results, but Bill does the hard work that will *create* better financial results.

WHICH WILL YOU BE?

If you look at Cal's and Bill's lofty CEO position and money earned, their *rewards* don't look different. But consider three phases in their *journeys* that might help you decide which to take.

CHAPTER 1: BUILDERS AND CLIMBERS

1. Contributor phase: Bill had more fun on the way up. He became a master at delivering value to customers and generating profitable, sustainable organic growth. Bill knew he was good at this, and those around him knew it. He showed up for work with purpose, and his subordinates joined him with enthusiasm.

Cal had less fun. His best hope for getting to the top was landing leadership positions in businesses that still had costs to cut and then jumping to his next business. His subordinates understood Cal's game. The decades Cal spent getting to the top were largely void of relaxed confidence, a sense of accomplishment, and earned respect from others.

- Engaging work
- Accomplishment
- Respect of peers

- Confidence
- Industry respect
- Loyal employees

- Teaching others
- Advising startups
- Keynote speaking

2. Leader phase: Life is different for Bill and Cal at the top. When Bill became CEO, he applied his tried-and-true growth model to every part of the company. His entire industry admires his company, and future Builders want to emulate him. Employees love to work for him because he values their contributions, and they're proud to be part of what's being built.

While Bill keeps building, Cal has nowhere left to climb. Now he's got to deliver, and he only knows one way to do this. Cut costs. Employees lose their jobs, families are uprooted, and future

INEXPLICABLY, CAL RECEIVES FINANCIAL REWARDS FROM HIS COMPANY FOR HARPOONING ITS FUTURE.

4

Builders jump ship. Inexplicably, Cal receives financial rewards from his company for harpooning its future. Cal gets his money, but not the respect of others.

3. Retirement phase: Few people consider the third phase—retirement. For the next couple of decades, Bill is in demand. Teach an executive MBA class at a prestigious university? Deliver keynote addresses at conferences? Join the board of a dynamic company? Advise a startup that's commercializing exciting new technology? Help a nonprofit bring aid to a poverty- or disease-stricken population? Bill gets to pick.

Cal simply fades away. Who needs a retired, cost-cutting Climber?

You may think getting to the top of your company is the finish line. For some, the goal may indeed be to *get mine and get out*. But don't forget to think about what you'll be doing *after* you get out.

And don't limit your thinking to what you'll *do* in retirement. You'll find satisfaction in looking back on what you *did*. As a Builder, you can leave an amazing legacy, positively impacting the lives of employees and their families, and quite possibly the world.

FOR WHOM IS THIS BOOK WRITTEN?

I hope this book will inspire those starting their careers. Yes, you can be a Builder by starting your own company, and that may indeed be your path. But you can also be an entrepreneur inside a large corporation—sometimes referred to as an "intrapreneur." Large companies need people like you, and you'll have the benefit of bringing enormous corporate resources to bear on your building projects.

I hope this book will embolden midcareer Builders. Has your

journey been driven solely by your internal compass? Have others failed to understand why you do what you do? Use what you learn in these pages to explain yourself to your leaders. Find out if their goals match yours. If not, *sprint* to another company that embraces Builders.

> **WHEN YOU PICK YOUR LEADERS, YOUR EMPLOYEES ARE WATCHING.**

I hope this book will guide boards of directors and C-level suites. Sure, my Cal and Bill examples are at the extremes on a continuum. But when you're selecting general managers, group VPs, and CEOs, you need to understand the underlying motivation that *drives* each candidate. Failing to do so can stall your growth trajectory and drive out your best future leaders.

This last point is critical. I've had dozens of conversations with employees after a new leader is appointed. If it's a Cal, many of the best performers start updating their resumes. Remember, when you pick your leaders, your employees are watching.

I hope this book will encourage those who never plan to be Builders. It takes a team to build a cathedral: quarry miners, architects, scaffold erectors, stain glass artisans. Join a business led by a Builder if you can. You'll enjoy being part of an exciting building program. And you'll be less likely to lose your job in a round of cost-cutting.

WHY SHOULD YOU READ THIS BOOK?

Together we'll explore the why and the how of business building. Research and logic will reveal *why* Builders are essential for your company. Our research includes a survey with 654 responses.[1] From this you'll see that businesses led by Builders are far more successful than others.

There's a simple logic to putting a Builder in charge: your company—and every company you can think of—was *founded* by a Builder. We'll explore a century-long evolution in management that has allowed non-Builders into leadership positions. You'll see the problems this has created and why they should be remedied.

The "how" of business building is two-fold, covering what Builders *should* do and what they *should not* do. You may be surprised at how many unforced errors senior leaders make today. We'll explore each and use our research to understand their negative impact.

Someday these errors will be clearly seen for what they are: self-inflicted decisions that do more to block healthy growth than bolster it. These errors are far too common among business leaders today. In fact, some leaders could boost business growth by staying home and doing nothing.

When you put Builders in charge and stop making these errors, your business will thrive. That's my hope for your business.

SOME LEADERS COULD BOOST BUSINESS GROWTH BY STAYING HOME AND DOING NOTHING.

CHAPTER 1: BUILDERS AND CLIMBERS

ABOUT OUR RESEARCH

Throughout this book, you'll see many references to our survey. It garnered 654 responses representing approximately ten thousand years of combined experience.

Responses came from three job levels: individual contributor, middle manager, and senior leader. Most questions asked about the behavior of senior leaders. These respondents hailed from companies with a broad range of annual revenues.

10,000 YEARS OF WORK EXPERIENCE
- <10 YEARS EXPERIENCE
- 10-20 YEARS
- 20-30 YEARS
- >30 YEARS

RESPONSES SORTED BY THREE JOB LEVELS
- INDIVIDUAL CONTRIBUTOR
- MIDDLE MANAGER
- SENIOR LEADER

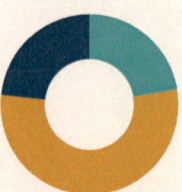

ANNUAL REVENUE OF COMPANIES
- <$50 MILLION
- $50-$500 MILLION
- $0.5-$2 BILLION
- $2-$5 BILLION
- >$5 BILLION

We saw very little difference in leadership behavior based on various firmographics. We explore the impact of these firmographics in chapter 11.

PRIVATELY HELD & PUBLICLY TRADED COMPANIES

- PUBLICLY TRADED
- PRIVATELY HELD

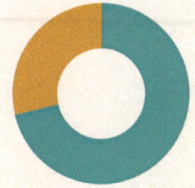

RESPONSES WEIGHTED TOWARD NORTH AMERICA

- NORTH AMERICA
- LATIN AMERICA
- EUROPE
- ASIA
- MIDDLE EAST/AFRICA

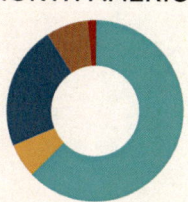

MANY RESPONSES FROM B2B COMPANIES

- B2B MATERIALS
- B2B COMPONENTS
- B2B EQUIPMENT
- B2B SERVICES
- B2C OFFERINGS

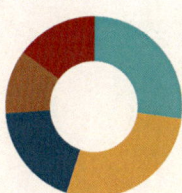

DIFFERING SELF-REPORTED GROWTH RATES

- SLOWER GROWTH
- SAME AS COMPETITORS
- FASTER GROWTH

CHAPTER 1: **BUILDERS AND CLIMBERS**

CHAPTER 2
WHAT IS A BUSINESS BUILDER?

> "There is only one definition of a leader. You must have followers."
>
> —PETER DRUCKER

CHAPTER 2: WHAT IS A BUSINESS BUILDER?

Your company, and every other company, was founded by a Builder. Builders can still be spotted. They drive profitable, sustainable growth by delivering differentiated value to customers,

BUILDERS DRIVE PROFITABLE, SUSTAINABLE GROWTH BY DELIVERING DIFFERENTIATED VALUE TO CUSTOMERS.

as they brush aside business fads, short-term distractions, and financial gymnastics. Under their leadership, the business grows in size, profitability, and stature.

But not every company is *still* led by Builders. Today, many senior leaders are Remodelers, Decorators, or Realtors.

REMODELERS, DECORATORS, AND REALTORS

Remodelers are forever fixing the place up. They may work on improving quality, boosting productivity, or eliminating wasteful costs. These are commendable endeavors, but if nothing new is built, the company reaps diminishing returns.

Imagine you've been working on quality improvements. Good! But what will you do after you get to zero defects? Perhaps you're driving down labor costs. You've finally reached full automation with a lights-out factory. Your productivity is fantastic, but what will you do next? You've reached diminishing returns.

REMODELING WITHOUT BUILDING IS A RACE TO THE BOTTOM THAT ENDS IN COMMODITIZATION.

Remodeling is good, but Remodeling without Building is a race to the bottom that ends in commoditization. Your competitors eventually match your quality or productivity with similar products. Now the price wars begin. Bottom line: keep Remodeling but never stop Building.

Decorators are always trying to boost "curb appeal." They're focused on how the place looks, and life is all about the quarterly financial report.

Decorators think they're doing meaningful work, but they aren't really making a difference. The energy they put into this quarter's financial report is squandered energy. Next year, no one will even remember that quarter that seemed so important at the time.

Remember Cal the Climber from chapter 1? Turns out that Climbers are often Decorators with a strong desire to look good in the near term.

Like Remodeling, there's nothing wrong with Decorating in itself: Why not look good to investors? The problem arises when Decorating occurs at the expense of Building. And it very often does, as many short-term actions to "look good" degrade long-term profitable growth.

You see, Decorators are engaged in a spectator sport, not a participant sport. The only way to change a quarterly financial

report in a *healthy* way—with sustainable revenue growth, premium pricing, and impressive profit margins—is to conduct strong Building in the years *prior* to the financial report.

> **DECORATORS PLAY THE LEAD ROLE IN A BUSINESS VERSION OF THE MOVIE *GROUNDHOG DAY*.**

Decorators play the lead role in a business version of the movie *Groundhog Day*. After each financial reporting period, they repeat the same activities all over again. Their business hasn't fundamentally changed. In fact, Decorators play a rather depressing version of *Groundhog Day*. Bill Murray's character at least used all those repetitions to build a better version of himself.

Realtors love to buy and sell, reaping their rewards during mergers and acquisitions. Realtors are rewarded when the hard work of *others'* hands is transferred into *their* hands. Realtors mostly redistribute wealth that others have created.

Research shows 70-90 percent of acquisitions fail.[2] But some *can* be helpful, especially when acquiring a competency that helps your business change its growth trajectory. When you have a Builder at the helm, the acquired business becomes a building block in her building program.

The problem with many Realtors is that they don't know how to grow what they acquire. Their acquisitions become enormous distractions from the Builder's work needed for organic growth. As a result, many Realtors are just building a house of cards.

Does this mean a business leader should forget about operational efficiency, financial reporting, or M&A? Of course not. But what is their *passion*? What gets them excited about their job? For the Builder, it's driving profitable, sustainable organic growth over the years by delivering differentiated value to customers.

IF YOU DON'T KNOW HOW TO GROW WHAT YOU ACQUIRE, YOU'RE JUST BUILDING A HOUSE OF CARDS.

HOW MANY LEADERS ARE BUILDERS?

To avoid bias in our survey, we didn't use these four terms: Builder, Remodeler, Decorator, and Realtor. We didn't think many leaders would cheerfully identify themselves as a Decorator. Instead, we asked respondents to characterize the behaviors of their companies' senior leaders using the four descriptions below. We added our four labels *after* the survey.

- Driving organic growth by delivering differentiated value to customers. (Builder)
- Improving operational efficiency through productivity, quality, and costs. (Remodeler)
- Presenting favorable financial performance and outlook to investors. (Decorator)
- Pursuing external alliances, including mergers and acquisitions. (Realtor)

WE ASKED RESPONDENTS TO IDENTIFY THE *PRIMARY PASSION* OF SENIOR LEADERS IN THEIR COMPANY.

We asked survey respondents to identify the *primary passion* of senior leaders in their company. Fifty-three percent of senior leaders gave themselves the Builder description, while only 32 percent of subordinates characterized their senior leaders this way.[3]

More subordinates thought of their senior leaders as Remodelers (41 percent) focused on operational efficiency. Remodeling work is is important, but it's *not* a path to profitable, sustainable growth.

WHY AREN'T THERE MORE BUILDERS?

It seems problematic that "driving growth by delivering differentiated value to customers" is the primary passion for only about one-third to one-half of senior leaders. How did we get here? Consider four possible reasons:

FOUR TYPES OF LEADERS

Have you ever completed a psychometric survey? Then you know it's rare for anyone to be characterized as 100 percent of one personality type.

The same is true for senior leaders. In fact, their role is so complex that they *must* bring a range of skills to bear on the problems they face.

But just like a psychometric study, every leader has a primary way of thinking. This *primary passion* is what the leader loves to do . . . what the leader has become very good at . . . what *defines* the leader.

LEADER TYPE	PRIMARY PASSION	PRIMARY TIMEFRAME	CHARACTERISTIC ACTIVITIES
Builder	Organic Growth	Years	• Focused on strategic markets • Voice of customer research • Strong R&D project portfolio
Remodeler	Operational Efficiency	Quarters	• Quality improvement • Productivity enhancement • Business process improvement
Decorator	Financial Reporting	Quarters	• Investor relations • Internal financial reviews • Cost-cutting programs
Realtor	M&A	Quarters	• Acquisition screening • M&A due diligence • M&A synergy capture

1. We don't have Builders among us anymore.
2. We don't need Builders leading well-established companies.
3. Business management and ownership structure has changed.
4. Builder "muscles" have atrophied and complacency has set in.

The first reason can be quickly dispatched. Yes, there were impressive Builders a century ago, but for every Edison, Ford, Carnegie, and Eastman, we now have a Gates, Jobs, Bezos, and Musk. Just as those earlier Builders had their critics, so do today's. I'm not endorsing all aspects of their behavior. I'm just suggesting entrepreneurship remains strong. We still have Builders among us.

> **ONCE A COMPANY IS ESTABLISHED, CAN WE SEND THE BUILDERS HOME AND TAKE IT FROM HERE?**

Consider the second reason: Once a company is established, maybe it can be safely handed over to other leaders lacking a Builder mentality. Perhaps we can send the Builders home and take it from here?

The complexities of running a large company indeed require skills the Founder-Builder may lack. But you should supplement—not supplant—your Builder leaders. How can any company facing competition maintain strong growth without aggressively meeting changing market needs? As our research will show, we may not have as many Builder leaders today, but we still need them.

The third explanation has merit: Business management and ownership structure have changed. Over the last century, we've moved from entrepreneurial capitalism to managerial capitalism to fiduciary capitalism.[4] As shown in the sidebar on page 21, this has reduced today's leaders' *motive* and *means* to grow their companies. No wonder many lack their founders' clarity of purpose.

The fourth reason is also valid, if disappointing. Perhaps you've seen this at your company: Someone developed an amazing

NOT SO MANY BUILDERS

In our survey, the Builder trait was described as "driving organic growth by delivering differentiated value to customers."

Fifty-three percent of senior leaders said this was their primary passion. But only 32 percent of subordinates thought this was their senior leaders' primary passion.

While every company was founded by a Builder, it seems only one-third to one-half of them are *still* led by Builders.

WHICH BEST DESCRIBES YOUR SENIOR LEADERS' PRIMARY PASSION?

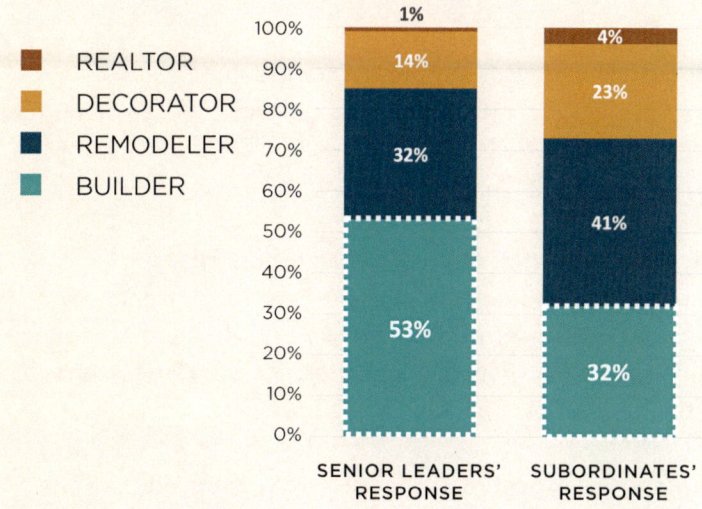

product line long ago that still generates outsized growth and profits for decades. What required blood, sweat and tears to *build* requires relatively little effort to *manage*. Managers make a comfortable living never realizing their success was pre-determined by earlier Builders. Builder muscles atrophy and complacency sets in.

> **MANAGERS MAKE A COMFORTABLE LIVING NEVER REALIZING THEIR SUCCESS WAS PRE-DETERMINED BY EARLIER BUILDERS.**

BUT MUST *LEADERS* BE BUILDERS?

Clearly a company needs to keep building—delivering differentiated products to its customers—if it is to profitably grow. But an honest question is, *Does the Builder role need to rest with our senior leaders?* To answer this, we turn to our research.

We asked all employees—individual contributors, middle management, and senior leaders this question: "Based on current leadership behavior, which best characterizes your company's prospects for future growth?"

We found that most of the companies expecting faster revenue growth—60 percent of them—had senior leaders who characterized themselves as Builders. For companies expecting the same or slower growth, only 19 percent were led by those selecting the Builder definition for themselves.

The companies expecting slower growth were mostly led (54 percent) by Remodelers. This should be cautionary for Remodelers fixated on operational efficiency. Your perceived disinterest in growth could set low growth expectations for your employees. If you're a Remodeler, consider your growth prospects versus a competitor led by a Builder brimming with employees expecting their company to grow.

MEANS AND MOTIVE TO GROW

In the early 1900s, founders exercised both ownership and control (entrepreneurial capitalism). By the 1930s, these roles began to split as professional managers were hired and ownership was diluted among stockholders (managerial capitalism).

In the 1970s, ownership concentrated in the hands of institutional investors, giving a measure of control to those with financial self-interests (fiduciary capitalism).

Because the companies' founders had ownership, they had the *motive* to build something of lasting value. With control, they had the *means* to do so. Both ownership and control have been diluted for today's leaders, reducing both their motive and their means.

	Entrepreneurial Capitalism	**Managerial Capitalism**	**Fiduciary Capitalism**
	1900s	1930s	1970s
LEADER:	Founder	Professional Managers	Professional Managers
OWNER:	Founder	Stockholders	Institutional Investors
CONTROL:	Founder	Professional Managers	Managers + Investors
LEADER'S POSITION:	Full means (control) and motive (ownership) to build the company	Full means but reduced motive to build the company	Reduced means and reduced motive to build the company

BUSINESS BUILDERS

We wondered if *expecting* growth and *achieving* growth might be two different things. As it turned out, though, more subordinates at Builder-led companies also reported they were *experiencing* faster-than-competition growth (41 percent) than those at Remodeler-led companies (27 percent).

DO YOU HAVE A BUILDER'S MINDSET?

Throughout this book you'll see how Builders *behave* and also what they *believe*. Business building is hard work and rarely takes place without firm convictions.

Do you have the mindset of a Builder? Find out by taking our (free) assessment at www.AreYouaBusinessBuilder.com. After completing it, you can download a personalized, confidential report that includes your Business Builder Score (max 100).

When you download your report, you may have questions as to *why* some beliefs are hallmarks of Business Builders. Your report will include explanations of these twenty Business Builder Beliefs, along with page references from this book for further exploration.

CHAPTER 3

BUILDERS EMBRACE THEIR FIRST DUTY

> "On matters of style, swim with the current, but on matters of principle, stand like a rock."
>
> —THOMAS JEFFERSON

CHAPTER 3: BUILDERS EMBRACE THEIR FIRST DUTY

What's the first duty of any business leader? It is this: leave your business stronger than you found it.

All stakeholders—shareholders, employees, customers, suppliers, and communities—benefit when a company's growth is not just strong and profitable but also

THE LEADER'S FIRST DUTY: LEAVE YOUR BUSINESS STRONGER THAN YOU FOUND IT.

sustainable. When growth is just unsustainable window dressing, only opportunistic leaders and opportunistic investors benefit.

A duty is a moral and/or legal obligation. It's a responsibility. Duty has also been described as a task one anticipates with distaste, performs with reluctance, and brags about afterward. In fact, fulfilling one's duty is seldom easy and often at odds with one's more immediate self-interests.

Whether you're a soldier, statesman, or spouse, you signed up for your duty. Same with the senior leader. Because it's a position of enormous influence, the duty of a senior leader deserves more careful consideration than many give it.

ONE LEADER'S DECISION CAN HAVE IRREVERSIBLE OUTCOMES FOR MANY.

The decisions of any senior leader can have an outsized impact beyond near-term financial results. Builders recognize the stone they toss in the pond may create waves, not ripples. One leader's decision can have irreversible outcomes for many:

- Hundreds of families are uprooted as employees are fired to improve current earnings.
- Your company's future is mortgaged by divesting long-term "crown jewel" technology.
- The future leader that could have taken your company to new heights left in disgust.
- Your century-old company sinks into irrelevance and must be acquired by another firm.

What does it mean to leave your business stronger than you found it? It means your company is better positioned to fulfill its mission, enjoy a strong growth trajectory, and meet the needs of *all* stakeholders.

The business leader's first duty is necessary, but it's not sufficient: Beyond leaving the business stronger, the leader has much else to achieve on their balanced scorecard.[5] But when a leader allows a business to stagnate or weaken—regardless of other achievements—that leader has failed.

> **WHEN A LEADER ALLOWS A BUSINESS TO STAGNATE OR WEAKEN, THAT LEADER HAS FAILED.**

WHEN THE FIRST DUTY IS IGNORED

In the 1980s, the company I worked for did something it had never done in its century-plus history. Under the euphemism "Overhead Value Analysis," the company had its first mass layoffs. (We called this "ova-and-out.") My company was not an outlier: right-sizing

CHAPTER 3: BUILDERS EMBRACE THEIR FIRST DUTY

swept industry after industry. Remarkably, the "right" size was always fewer, not more employees.

The last two decades of the 1900s were exemplified by two leaders. One CEO guided his company's value from $14 billion to $600 billion in twenty years.[6] *Fortune* magazine named him the Manager of the Century, and *Financial Times* named his company the World's Most Respected Company for three straight years.

> **REMARKABLY, THE "RIGHT" SIZE WAS ALWAYS *FEWER*, NOT MORE EMPLOYEES.**

Contrast that with a CEO about whom a book was recently written. The book is titled *The Man Who Broke Capitalism* and its subtitle claims this man *Gutted the Heartland and Crushed the Soul of Corporate America*.[7]

These CEOs are one and the same: Jack Welch. From his rise to CEO of General Electric in 1981 to his 2001 retirement, his ability to impress shareholders made him a business celebrity. Business leaders everywhere marveled at his ability to push GE's stock price ever higher. Most wanted to emulate him.

How did Welch accomplish this? Under his leadership, GE

- relentlessly downsized, eliminating 10 percent of its employees every year from 1981-2001.[8]
- "financialized" itself, with GE Capital contributing half of the company's profits at its peak.[9]
- vigorously pursued outsourcing and offshoring.[10]
- embarked on one of the country's most aggressive stock buyback programs.[11]
- unleashed an M&A boom, with nearly a thousand acquisitions.[12]
- engaged in "creative accounting" practices, prior to their ban with the 2002 Sarbanes-Oxley Act.[13]

As the world watched GE's stock rise, the company founded by Thomas Edison was being forever changed from within. GE had introduced or popularized light bulbs, electric motors, the x-ray machine, radios, television, moldable plastics, and America's first jet engine. Now industrial manufacturing and innovation were de-emphasized.

GE had been known as "Generous Electric." In 1962, one leader stated, "Maximizing employment security is a prime company goal." Their 1953 annual report proudly described all the many ways that GE worked "in the balanced best interests of all."[14]

THE COMPANY FOUNDED BY THOMAS EDISON WAS BEING FOREVER CHANGED FROM WITHIN.

BUSINESS BUILDERS

Did Jack Welch fulfill his first duty? By any measure, he did not leave his company stronger than he found it:

- Employee loyalty became a thing of the past, as hundreds of thousands lost their jobs.[15]
- The continual flow of innovation that had set GE apart dropped to a trickle.
- GE's extensive "financial engineering" left the company highly vulnerable to the 2008 recession.
- Twenty years after Welch's retirement, GE's value was only about one-quarter of its peak.

Think about that last point: even the single metric that Jack Welch relentlessly focused on—share price—was ultimately weakened by his efforts.

And the carnage was not limited to GE. Dozens of GE executives went on to manage other companies, including 3M, Home Depot, Boeing, Albertson's, Equifax, Medtronic, Stanley Works, Nielsen, Rubbermaid, and more. At many of these companies—and others emulating GE—the pattern continued. Builders were replaced, companies were weakened instead of strengthened, and many stakeholders eventually suffered.

> **EVEN THE SINGLE METRIC THAT JACK WELCH RELENTLESSLY FOCUSED ON—SHARE PRICE—WAS ULTIMATELY WEAKENED BY HIS EFFORTS.**

At the heart of this problem are two false goals. First, the false *company* goal of maximizing shareholder value, which we'll explore in chapter 4. Second, the false *personal* goal of a retirement "finish line," the topic of the next section.

WHEN THE FIRST DUTY IS FORGOTTEN

No one had ever seen anything like Jack Welch's twenty-year CEO reign at GE. Named by *Fortune* magazine as the Manager of the Century, he was revered for his ability to boost GE's stock price. What happened after he retired?

It was a grand illusion. Twenty years after Welch's reign, GE had still not recovered in terms of its market value—the very thing Welch had pursued.

More important, this company founded by Thomas Edison lost its Builder mentality. The blind pursuit of shareholder wealth led to a loss of innovation, manufacturing leadership, employee loyalty, growth capabilities, and industry reputation.

Jack Welch and the many leaders that emulated him failed in their first duty as a leader: *Leave your business stronger than you found it.*

GENERAL ELECTRIC STOCK PRICE, USD

CHAPTER 3: BUILDERS EMBRACE THEIR FIRST DUTY

NO FINISH LINE

Some senior leaders think of their retirement as the finish line. That's because they are thinking of themselves, not their first duty.

In *The Infinite Game*, Simon Sinek contrasts infinite games with finite games.[16] In finite games, like soccer, known players follow the same rules over a fixed time. Infinite games, like business, allow new players to enter the game and apply unorthodox methods. And they never end.

Did your company's founder envision a "finish line" for the company? If not, then why are senior leaders today imagining their retirement is the finish line? Instead of crossing a finish line, leaders should focus on passing the baton in a never-ending relay race.

LEADERS SHOULD FOCUS ON PASSING THE BATON IN A *NEVER-ENDING* RELAY RACE.

Did your last CEO understand their first duty was to leave the business stronger? Here's a clue: Which theme was central in their departure speech?

- A. "Over the last 'x' years we have accomplished the following. . ." (Where 'x' coincidentally matches this CEO's tenure.)
- B. "My friends, we are positioned so that the very best years of our company lie before us, because. . ."

If you serve on the board of directors, try this thought experiment when selecting your next CEO: upon retirement, which candidates will likely deliver speech A and which speech B?

NO LAUREL WREATH EITHER

A chief technology officer of a multi-billion-dollar company told me this story: A group president at his company said he "didn't believe in innovation." As you can imagine, this was rather alarming to a CTO in charge of innovation. The group president explained that he was retiring in two more years, and any innovation investment now wouldn't help him in time.

This group president had apparently simplified his business decision-making to, *What's in it for me?* Perhaps he no longer saw himself as another employee of the company. Maybe he thought he had "won" his position of influence, that this was something he deserved along with any related bounty he could accumulate.

This sounds like a severe case of managerial malpractice, but at least this group president was honest. He used his "outside voice" to explain his decision-making. How many business leaders only use their "inner voice" with this reasoning but still *behave* as this group president did?

CHAPTER 3: BUILDERS EMBRACE THEIR FIRST DUTY

I have no idea, and neither do you. Our accounting systems don't hold business leaders accountable to their first duty. This is a problem we'll address in chapter 9.

It's never too early in your career to make sure you've got the right mindset. If you're working your way up through your company, don't think of your new position as a gift you've been handed or a prize you've earned.

You haven't been handed a laurel wreath. You've been handed a trowel. What will you build with it? How will you leave your business stronger than you found it?

LEADERS HAVE NOT BEEN HANDED A LAUREL WREATH.

YOU'VE BEEN HANDED A TROWEL. WHAT WILL YOU BUILD WITH IT?

BUSINESS BUILDERS

CHAPTER 3: BUILDERS EMBRACE THEIR FIRST DUTY

TOM WILLIAMS

No one had to explain his first duty to Tom Williams. Tom was CEO of Parker Hannifin Corporation (NYSE:PH), a Fortune 250 global leader in motion and control technologies for eight years. During his tenure, EBITDA margins increased every year, from 14.7 percent to 22.6 percent.

While many retiring CEOs would dwell fondly on this, in our interview Tom was clearly more excited about how his company was *positioned for the future*.

The Parker team focused intently on market-facing innovation. Tom coined the phrase, "must-have products" to describe the differentiated Parker products customers *needed*.

The company trained over one thousand engineers in advanced interviewing methods to *understand customers' needs*. As a result, Parker's percent of sales from new products more than doubled.

Tom speaks passionately about engaging team members so they feel "ownership," comparing it to moving from a rented apartment to owning your first home. He said: "Team member engagement is the rising tide that lifts the entire boat."

His message was that your last name doesn't need to be Parker and that everyone can be a founder in their own way. The connection to the company's one hundred-plus years roots is so strong that every team member is encouraged to be a "refounder."

CHAPTER 4

BUILDERS AVOID FALSE GOALS

> "In the short term, the stock market is a voting machine. In the long term, it's a weighing machine."
>
> —BENJAMIN GRAHAM

CHAPTER 4: BUILDERS AVOID FALSE GOALS

Business leaders need to articulate a clear business goal that is shared by their organization. Lewis Carroll cautioned, "If you don't know where you are going, any road will get you there." The successful business leader needs everyone on the *right* road and on the *same* road.

As you saw in the last chapter, maximizing shareholder wealth became the primary goal for General Electric and many other companies. How did this come about?

In the 1970s, University of Chicago economist Milton Friedman promoted the idea that companies should focus exclusively on the profitable production of goods and services. He believed that the profit motive was a perfect sorting mechanism to cull good ideas from bad, and thus would benefit society at large.

Friedman went on to win the Nobel Prize in economics in 1976, and others advanced his theory. Professors Michael Jensen and William Meckling argued there was only one metric by which a corporation should be judged: its share price.

Some argued that boosting shareholder wealth was *the* overriding moral obligation of a leader. In fairness to Jack Welch, these were the prevailing winds when he became CEO in 1981.

SOME ARGUED THAT BOOSTING SHAREHOLDER WEALTH WAS THE OVERRIDING MORAL OBLIGATION OF A LEADER.

To what extent is this goal still popular today? Survey respondents were asked to identify their business's primary goal, given four options:

1. Maximize shareholder wealth
2. Beat competitors' performance
3. Grow by meeting customer needs
4. Meet the needs of all stakeholders

How popular was the first goal, maximizing shareholder wealth? Thirty-eight percent of senior leaders at publicly traded companies still see this as their company's primary goal.

There are three reasons why maximizing shareholder wealth is *not* a worthy goal for your company:

1. It's a lovely result, but a lousy goal.
2. It hasn't worked.
3. It defies investor logic.

REASON 1: IT'S A LOVELY RESULT, BUT A LOUSY GOAL.

Employees' goals should be actionable and inspiring. Maximizing shareholder value is neither. If a leader says the goal is to raise earnings per share this quarter, most employees will be clueless on how to help. This goal isn't actionable for them. But other goals—growing by meeting customer needs or beating the competition—could be actionable for many.

> **EMPLOYEES' GOALS SHOULD BE ACTIONABLE AND INSPIRING. MAXIMIZING SHAREHOLDER VALUE IS NEITHER.**

Maximizing shareholder wealth is hardly inspiring. In fact, it's common for employees hearing stock price or earning-per-share targets to become cynical about the leader's motivation. Is this just about the bosses getting their bonuses and stock options?

In a 2009 interview with the *Financial Times*, Jack Welch renounced shareholder value as a goal or strategy. And he made the point that shareholder value is indeed a *result*. He said, "On the face of it, shareholder value is the dumbest idea in the world. Shareholder value is a result, not a strategy. . . . Your main constituencies are your employees, your customers, and your products."[17]

REASON 2: IT HASN'T WORKED.

We wanted to know if higher-performing companies set different goals than lower-performing companies. So we asked senior leaders—the ones setting the goals—to identify their primary goal.

Then we compared responses from publicly traded companies where respondents said they were growing faster than competitors to those citing slower growth than competitors.[18] As shown in the sidebar, 32 percent of the senior leaders at faster-growth companies said their primary goal was maximizing shareholder wealth. At slower-growth companies, 70 percent of senior leaders said maximizing shareholder wealth was their primary goal.

> **AT SLOWER-GROWTH COMPANIES, 70 PERCENT OF SENIOR LEADERS SAID MAXIMIZING SHAREHOLDER WEALTH WAS THEIR PRIMARY GOAL.**

This shows correlation—not causation—but it hardly recommends maximizing shareholder wealth as a company goal. While maximizing shareholder wealth was the top goal at slower-growth companies, the top goal at faster-growth companies was to grow by meeting customer needs (49 percent).

Our survey findings are consistent with historical results. In a landmark *Harvard Business Review* article, Roger Martin analyzed shareholder returns from two time periods:[19]

- 1933–1976, when the prevailing view was that professional managers should pursue the interests of all stakeholders.
- 1977–2008, when it was widely accepted that the primary goal of business was to maximize shareholder wealth.

CHOOSE YOUR GOAL CAREFULLY

We asked senior leaders at publicly traded companies to identify one of four goals as their company's primary goal.

Then we compared the responses from companies that respondents said were growing faster than competition to those growing slower than competition.

By far, the most popular company goal for slower-growth companies was to maximize shareholder wealth. For faster-growth companies, the top goal was to grow by meeting customer needs.

SENIOR LEADERS: WHICH BEST DESCRIBES YOUR PRIMARY BUSINESS GOAL?

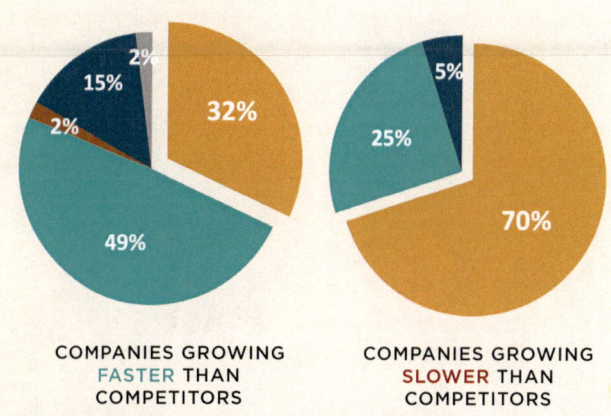

COMPANIES GROWING FASTER THAN COMPETITORS

COMPANIES GROWING SLOWER THAN COMPETITORS

- MAXIMIZE SHAREHOLDER WEALTH
- GROW BY MEETING CUSTOMER NEEDS
- BEAT COMPETITORS
- SATISFY ALL STAKEHOLDERS
- UNSURE

BUSINESS BUILDERS

CHAPTER 4: BUILDERS AVOID FALSE GOALS

In the 1933–1976 period, shareholders of the S&P 500 earned compound annual real returns of 7.6 percent. From 1977 to the end of 2008, they did much worse, earning real returns of only 5.9 percent a year. Certainly there were other economic forces at play over these decades. But an intense three-decade focus on boosting shareholder wealth didn't seem to work.

REASON 3: IT DEFIES INVESTOR LOGIC.

This may seem counterintuitive, but when you understand how a publicly traded company is valued, it should *discourage* you from focusing on the stock price, at least in the near term.

Imagine a company has current year earnings of $1 billion and a price-to-earnings ratio of 20, leading to a market valuation of $20 billion. This means $19 billion—95 percent of the company's value—is driven by something *other* than this year's earnings.

What is it? It's the market's expectations of future growth. For most companies, by far the largest component of its value is determined by what investors think that company will do in the future, not today.

WHAT DRIVES A COMPANY'S SHAREHOLDER VALUE?

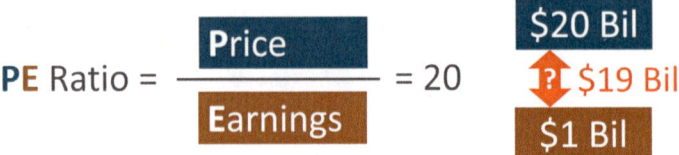

What determines the stock **price** of this company?
5% is from earnings performance **THIS YEAR**.
95% comes from expectations of **FUTURE GROWTH**.

Sadly, many business leaders focus on this year's earnings (the 5 percent), hit the reset button next year, focus on that current year, and repeat. This gives them little leverage to change their future, compared to leaders focused on future growth (the 95 percent).

Paradoxically, *focusing* on shareholder value distracts leaders from *impacting* shareholder value. Those fluctuating stock prices are highly distorted measures of a company's true value, more accurately reflecting the moods and tactics of traders. If you try to satisfy those traders *and* build the long-term value of your company, you'll find yourself aiming at two very different targets. This isn't a winning strategy.

> **PARADOXICALLY, *FOCUSING* ON SHAREHOLDER VALUE DISTRACTS LEADERS FROM *IMPACTING* SHAREHOLDER VALUE.**

We've moved from an era of shareholders to share *handlers*, with the average holding time now down to mere months.[20] Are these really the people senior leaders need to please? Builders don't owe any allegiance to those who feel no allegiance to them. Builders focus on what they are building, not the fickle crowds watching them work.

To be clear, it's not misguided to seek increases in long-term shareholder value. In fact, that's precisely the *result* that Builders accomplish. It's a matter of timing. Jeff Bezos said it well: "If you're long-term oriented, customer interests and shareholder interests are aligned. In the short term, that's not always the case."

CHAPTER 4: BUILDERS AVOID FALSE GOALS

FOR WHOM DO YOU RUN?

Imagine you're running a 10,000-meter race and a spectator in the stands has placed a side bet on your time for running lap #17 of 25.

Would you sprint lap #17 for all you're worth, sacrificing your long race so this spectator can win their one-lap bet? The spectator cares not a whit about your longer-term success.

Neither do those investors that hold your company's stock for mere months. Run for your company, not for them.

WOULD YOU SACRIFICE YOUR LONG RACE SO A SPECTATOR CAN WIN HIS ONE-LAP BET?

CHAPTER 5
BUILDERS DRIVE PROFITABLE, SUSTAINABLE GROWTH

> "You can hold a rock concert or you can hold a ballet. Just don't hold a rock concert and advertise it as a ballet."
>
> —WARREN BUFFETT

CHAPTER 5: BUILDERS DRIVE PROFITABLE, SUSTAINABLE GROWTH

If maximizing shareholder wealth is a poor goal, what's a better one? Where does profitable, sustainable growth, the topic of this chapter, fit in the picture? Is it just one of the three goals in the triple bottom line: social, environmental, and economic (people, planet, and profits)? Or does it play a larger role?

In the last chapter, we saw that oversimplifying the company goal to one edict—*maximize shareholder wealth*—causes problems. It's too complicated for that. It's more helpful to think of nesting three concepts: purpose, goal, and competency. Like Matryoshka dolls, each is unique, but all must fit together.

Your company's purpose is why it exists. In *Start with Why*, Simon Sinek showed how leaders inspire others by first explaining *why* they are in business.[21] Examples of mission or vision statements—each unique to its company—include:

- Airbnb: Creating a world where anyone can belong anywhere.
- Tesla: Accelerating the world's transition to sustainable energy.

44

- Uber: Reimagining the way the world moves for the better.
- Nike: Bringing inspiration and innovation to every athlete in the world.

While every company will have its own unique *purpose*, most companies will do well with the same *goal*: profitable, sustainable growth. What *competency* will let them achieve this? Market-facing innovation. We'll explore profitable, sustainable growth in this chapter and market-facing innovation in the next.

WHY PROFITABLE, SUSTAINABLE GROWTH?

What do we mean by growth that is profitable and sustainable?

- Growth: Your top-line revenue increases at a strong annual rate.
- Profitable: Your margins provide ample funding for future investment.
- Sustainable: You can maintain this healthy growth indefinitely.

Within the context of your purpose or mission, I encourage you to make such growth your primary goal for one reason: *all* stakeholders benefit from profitable, sustainable growth. Consider what can take place when you achieve it.

> ***ALL* STAKEHOLDERS BENEFIT FROM PROFITABLE, SUSTAINABLE GROWTH.**

Employees: There's less need to worry about layoffs for two reasons. First, the company has the financial resilience to weather economic downturns. Second, it has attracted long-term investors that don't *want* short-term actions that damage long-term health.

Senior leaders: The leadership team can spend more time building the business and less time attracting and appeasing investors. Activist investors become active at other companies, not their own.

Customers: Customers want to buy from such a company. It's growing because it is reliably meeting the needs of these customers with high-quality, innovative products and services.

ESG interests: The company has the financial means to invest in environmental, social, and governance initiatives (e.g., waste management, renewable energy, human rights, employee diversity, etc.)

Communities: The company can invest where its employees and their families live. It's unlikely these communities will be devastated by the closing of their factories and offices.

Suppliers: The company's strong, reliable growth supports not only its own employees, but it also provides stable income to many suppliers and their employees.

Investors: Investors are well rewarded. Nothing increases the value of a company like the promise of a bright future. For the investor, a bright future *is* profitable, sustainable growth.

It may be obvious that profitable, sustainable growth is important, but why is it so hard to achieve? Why is it so rare to see a company generating outsized, profitable growth in a reliable, consistent fashion year after year?

There are two reasons such growth is more difficult than many realize. The first is the Red Queen Effect, and the second we call the Three Types of Growth. Let's explore both, not to discourage you but to demonstrate why Builders must pursue this type of growth so aggressively.

THE RED QUEEN EFFECT

Imagine your business is developing next year's operating plan, and you're considering a specific market. Someone says, "This market is growing at 3 percent annually, so we should be able to grow our sales here by 5 percent next year."

Of course, your competitors are having similar meetings. How fast do you think they're planning to grow in this market—the same, higher, or lower than the market growth rate? Also higher, right?

This means all the suppliers plan to grow faster than the market they serve. As TV psychologist Dr. Phil, might say, *How's that been working for you?* Why will you win, while they lose? How will you move faster than the world around you? This dilemma is called the Red Queen Effect. In *Alice in Wonderland* by Lewis Carroll, Alice had to run as fast as she could just to stay in place.

RED QUEEN EFFECT

"HERE WE MUST RUN AS FAST AS WE CAN, JUST TO STAY IN PLACE."
—LEWIS CARROLL

What are you doing that lets you "run faster" than competitors? Is your R&D staff 20 percent brighter? Is your marketing team

CHAPTER 5: BUILDERS DRIVE PROFITABLE, SUSTAINABLE GROWTH

more persuasive? Is your sales force harder working? Can you think of even *one* unassailable competitive advantage? You need something if you want your business to rise above mediocrity.

THREE TYPES OF GROWTH

Imagine you need to estimate your business growth rate for next year. You grew 5 percent this year, so maybe next year you'll shoot for 8 percent growth. After all you *did* grow your business 5 percent, right? Well, not really. You see, there are three types of growth: inherited growth, market growth, and earned growth. And you only control one of them: earned growth.

Inherited growth comes from differentiated products created by clever employees at your company long ago. Look around your business right now. You probably see some legacy product

MOST BUSINESS LEADERS TAKE CREDIT FOR INHERITED, UNEARNED GROWTH.

platforms that continue to deliver outsized profitability and growth. These are the gifts that keep giving. Until they don't.

In the 1990s, my job was to market a polymer one of our company's scientists had invented in the 1950s. It was a key ingredient in many skincare products, and our profit margins were ridiculously high. We couldn't take credit for this, but we knew we needed to protect this "crown jewel" with ongoing innovation and patents.

Your competitors are trying to match your legacy products, and your customers *want* your competitors to succeed. As soon as competitors duplicate your product, your customers' purchasing agents will speed-dial you and demand lower pricing.

FOR EARNED GROWTH, YOU MUST UNDERSTAND AND MEET CUSTOMER NEEDS BETTER THAN OTHERS.

Most business leaders take credit for this inherited, unearned growth. And they take it for granted. It's better to think of these legacy products as sandcastles on the shore. The only question is *when*—not if—competitors will knock them down.

Market growth is the second type of unearned growth. Like inherited growth, you don't control it. You'll grow at the same rate as the market if your products are average—a kind word for mediocre—in the value they deliver.

Think of market growth as the tide that lifts and lowers all boats. Don't take market growth for granted. If your competitor launches a great new product, you could experience negative growth. No more rising tide for you.

Earned growth is the only growth that you control. Earned growth takes place under one and only one condition: you understand and meet customer needs better than others.

CHAPTER 5: **BUILDERS DRIVE PROFITABLE, SUSTAINABLE GROWTH**

THREE TYPES OF GROWTH

If your business grew at a 5 percent rate, it's possible you only "earned" a small part of that growth, if any. There are three components to growth, and the first two are "unearned."

Inherited growth is the outsized growth you enjoy from legacy product platforms that continue to demonstrate competitive advantage.

Market growth is what you get from supplying a market with products of average value.

Earned growth is achieved when you understand and meet customer needs better than others. This is the growth Builders pursue.

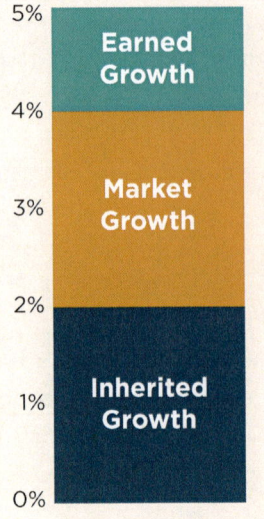

Earned Growth — When you understand and meet customer needs better than others.

Market Growth — When your products deliver the same value as competitors.

Inherited Growth — When your older, legacy products keep delivering outsized growth.

Given (a) the Red Queen Effect and (b) the illusion of growth that was in fact unearned, we know profitable, sustainable growth is hard. Beyond this, many senior leaders haven't even made it a top priority. In our research, only 53 percent of senior leaders said their primary passion was *driving organic growth by delivering differentiated value to customers*. That's the bad news.

The good news is you can boost your organic growth by simply halting some self-inflicted practices. Our research reveals several unforced errors commonly made by companies today. These include short time horizons, improperly prioritized initiatives, overuse of near-term cost controls, and a fixation on financial reporting. We'll examine each in subsequent chapters.

But ultimately, the key competency that will deliver the profitable, sustainable growth you desire is market-facing innovation. We'll use *market-facing innovation* as shorthand for delivering products and services with superior, differentiated value to customers. This is what the founder(s) of your company did so well. This is what Builders do today. And this is the subject of our next chapter.

CHAPTER 5: **BUILDERS DRIVE PROFITABLE, SUSTAINABLE GROWTH**

CHAPTER 6

BUILDERS PURSUE MARKET-FACING INNOVATION

> "Making products for your customers is far more efficient than finding customers for your products."
>
> —SETH GODIN

CHAPTER 6: BUILDERS PURSUE MARKET-FACING INNOVATION

In the last chapter, we said market-facing innovation is shorthand for delivering superior, differentiated value to customers. Think of it as new product development, where customers get new benefits and the term *product* is broadly applied. If a banker or insurance agent says they have a new product for you, they're including services, and so shall we.

A common precursor to product development is exploratory innovation through research, open innovation, alliances, ventures, etc. Many call their exploratory innovation "technology development." It fills the pantry shelf with useful ingredients, and then product development uses these ingredients to create an offering of value.

Technology development (exploratory innovation) and product development (market-facing innovation) are closely linked but quite different. Technology development turns money into knowledge, and product development turns knowledge back into money.

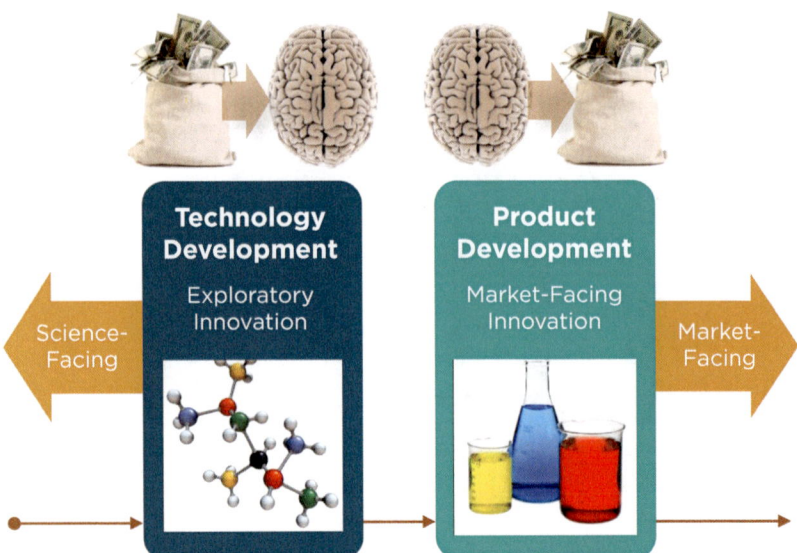

INNOVATION IS BASED ON SCIENCE THAT EVENTUALLY FLOWS TO MARKETS.

In the last chapter, I described a decades-old polymer made for skincare products by the chemical company I worked at. To keep competitors at bay, we invested heavily in new *technology development* for making this polymer: we were turning money into knowledge as we learned how to do this.

Finally, it was time to start creating specific products for each market we served. With this successful *product development*, we then turned our knowledge back into money with premium product pricing.

TECHNOLOGY DEVELOPMENT TURNS MONEY INTO KNOWLEDGE, AND PRODUCT DEVELOPMENT TURNS KNOWLEDGE BACK INTO MONEY.

Companies don't decide how much to invest in technology development and product development in a vacuum. They consider other initiatives such as productivity improvements and sales force training. Our survey asked respondents how senior leaders allocate resources among six types of initiatives:

1. Market-facing innovation (product development)
2. Exploratory innovation (technology development)
3. Marketing and sales capabilities
4. Productivity and quality improvements
5. Mergers and acquisitions
6. Other

On average, senior leaders allocate 24 percent of their resources to market-facing innovation and 16 percent to exploratory innovation. Is a combined total of 40 percent for these two sufficient? Respondents from companies experiencing faster growth than competitors invested more (43 percent), while those growing slower invested less (36 percent). We can't say what the "right" amount is, but we'll argue it should be the *most important* initiative for your company.

CHAPTER 6: BUILDERS PURSUE MARKET-FACING INNOVATION

Market-facing innovation is what Builders do to achieve profitable, sustainable growth. Here are three reasons to make market-facing innovation *your* predominant focus.

1. This is what exceptional companies do.
2. We're now in the Innovation Wave.
3. Nothing else drives reliable growth.

REASON 1: THIS IS WHAT EXCEPTIONAL COMPANIES DO.

For their book, *The Three Rules*, authors Michael Raynor and Mumtaz Ahmed analyzed data on over 25,000 companies spanning forty-five years.[22] From this, they identified 344 companies with truly exceptional performance. After extensive analysis, they were able to identify a small set of rules used at these companies, but not at lower-performing companies. These exceptional companies followed three rules.

THESE EXCEPTIONAL COMPANIES FOLLOWED THREE RULES.

Rule #1

Better before cheaper.

Rule #2

Revenue before cost.

Rule #3

There are no other rules.

Source: *The Three Rules*, by Michael Raynor and Mumtaz Ahmed

HOW DO LEADERS ALLOCATE RESOURCES?

On average, senior leaders allocate just 24 percent of their resources to market-facing innovation (product development).

They spend another 16 percent of their resources on exploratory innovation (technology development), which serves to feed their market-facing innovation.

More resources are devoted to these two types of innovation at companies growing faster than competition (43 percent) than companies growing slower (36 percent).

HOW DO SENIOR LEADERS IN YOUR COMPANY ALLOCATE RESOURCES TO THESE GROWTH INITIATIVES?

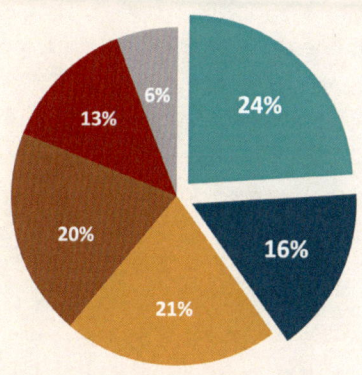

- MARKET-FACING INNOVATION
- EXPLORATORY INNOVATION
- MARKETING & SALES CAPABILITIES
- PRODUCTIVITY & QUALITY
- MERGERS & ACQUISITIONS
- OTHER

First, better before cheaper. A company needs to compete on both price and non-price factors, such as product performance, durability, etc. Their research showed the exceptional companies competed more on *non-price factors*, while low performers competed more on price.

The second rule is revenue before cost. Return on assets has been shown to be a good measure of profitability.[23] It can be boosted by increasing revenue (the numerator) or by decreasing assets or costs (the denominator). Relative to the low performers, exceptional companies were more likely to improve returns by generating more revenue, not by lowering their costs.

> **THE THIRD RULE? THERE ARE NO OTHER RULES. THERE ARE ONLY TWO COMMON RULES FOR SUCCESS.**

The third rule? There are no other rules. The authors weren't trying to be amusing. They found that while there are some unique ways to win, there are *only* two common rules for success.

So be wary if someone on your team wants to compete on price, or thinks becoming the low-cost producer is the best path to success. This research affirms the natural inclination of the Builder: use market-facing innovation to make products customers love (better before cheaper), and from this drive profitable, sustainable growth (revenue before costs).

REASON 2: WE'RE NOW IN THE INNOVATION WAVE.

Here's a second reason to focus on market-facing innovation: We're in a particularly good season for this now. This wasn't always true. When many companies had terrible product quality and inefficient operations, it made sense to focus on those shortcomings.

Consider three waves: the Quality Wave, the Productivity Wave, and the Innovation Wave. In the middle of the twentieth century, Dr. W. Edwards Deming told American business leaders they should rely on statistics rather than inspectors to improve quality. He showed how statistical process control charting could limit unwanted variation in upstream production well before any final inspection. They ignored him, so in the 1950s he convinced a small Japanese company called Toyota to use his methods. And so began the Quality Wave.

BEING EARLY OR LATE FOR A WAVE HAS CONSEQUENCES.

Other Japanese manufacturers quickly emulated Toyota's methods, and between 1960 and 1980, Japanese global automotive market share increased from 3 percent to nearly 30 percent.[24] The point is, being early or late for a wave has consequences. Same with the Productivity Wave, with its lean manufacturing and business process redesign.

MANY GENERALS HAVE BEEN GUILTY OF PLANNING FOR THE LAST WAR.

Don't plan for the last war | Plan forward

Quality Wave | Productivity Wave | Innovation Wave

BUSINESS BUILDERS

This is also true for the Innovation Wave, but there's a difference: the first two waves applied to current operations, so they reached a point of diminishing returns. What do you do next if you have zero defects or a fully automated factory?

The Innovation Wave impacts future sales, so it has unlimited potential. Figure this out and you reach that holy grail of business: profitable, sustainable growth.

The key is to plan forward. Many generals have been guilty of planning for the last war. Quality and productivity improvements are fine, but they were the last century's war. The Innovation Wave promises to be exciting and rewarding. To benefit from it, you need to be the next Toyota in your industry, not the next Chrysler.

My first rule of battle is *you can't win one you don't know you are in*. Let's be clear: today's battleground is the Innovation Wave, and the key to winning is superior market-facing innovation.

REASON 3: NOTHING ELSE DRIVES PROFITABLE SUSTAINABLE GROWTH.

Senior leaders have many initiatives to choose from, but only market-facing innovation can lead to profitable, sustainable growth. Consider how each of these popular initiatives falls short of such growth.

- **Productivity increases** can improve profitability, but they don't impact the revenue line needed for *growth*. They help profitability, but a point of diminishing returns is eventually reached, blocking the sustainability of such initiatives.
- **Quality improvements** may help revenue growth, but not to the extent they did a few decades ago: Today, reliable quality is usually considered table stakes. And as with productivity, a point of diminishing returns is reached, preventing sustainability.

WELCOME TO THE INNOVATION WAVE

Companies used to achieve competitive advantage by being first in the Quality Wave or Productivity Wave. Quality and productivity improvements still help, but are no longer major differentiators.

Since quality and productivity impact current operations, they reach a point of diminishing returns. What do you do *after* you reach zero defects or full automation?

Not so with the Innovation Wave, which impacts future sales. It has unlimited potential.

Latecomers to the first two waves faced poor financial results. Latecomers to the Innovation Wave face extinction.

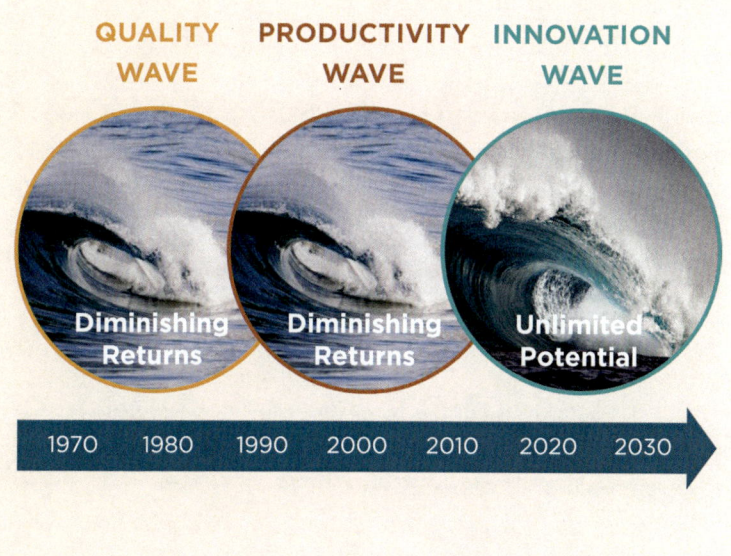

CHAPTER 6: BUILDERS PURSUE MARKET-FACING INNOVATION

- **Cost reductions** are like productivity increases in that they don't impact revenue growth and reach diminishing returns. Carelessly applied, they can damage a business's growth capabilities and have a negative—not neutral—effect on growth.

- **Sales training** is a popular initiative that can boost revenue growth *and* lead to better pricing for increased profitability. But it lacks sustainability: if a business doesn't keep delivering *new* value, customers will eventually buy from competitors' well-trained salespeople.

- **Acquisitions** will boost revenue and perhaps profits. But if the business doesn't know how to grow the companies it acquires, it's just building an unsustainable house of cards.

The common shortfall is a lack of *sustainable* growth. Not so with market-facing innovation. If a business understands and meets market needs better than others, its growth will be strong, profitable, *and sustainable*.

> IF A BUSINESS UNDERSTANDS AND MEETS MARKET NEEDS BETTER THAN OTHERS, ITS GROWTH WILL BE STRONG, PROFITABLE, *AND SUSTAINABLE.*

Many initiatives are needed for a well-balanced business. But senior leaders shouldn't treat all initiatives the same. As Stephen Covey noted, "The main thing is to keep the main thing the main thing." For companies seeking profitable, sustainable growth, the main thing is market-facing innovation.

Peter Drucker noted the primacy of market-facing innovation by saying a business's only basic functions are marketing and innovation. You're in business to understand and meet customers' needs, which are largely managed by the marketing and innovation functions, respectively.

I've heard leaders say, "Last year we implemented productivity improvements, and this year we're going to focus on market insight for better innovation." Market-facing innovation shouldn't

THE *ONLY* INITIATIVE FOR RELIABLE GROWTH

There are many possible initiatives senior leaders can pursue. But if the target is profitable, sustainable growth, nearly all miss the target.

The only one that can deliver this growth is market-facing innovation. Some initiatives, like productivity increases or cost reductions, don't impact the top revenue line at all, so they can't affect growth.

Others—like sales training—impact the revenue line but are not sustainable. If you don't keep delivering *new* value to your customers, they'll start buying from someone else's well-trained sales reps.

Can this initiative deliver...	revenue growth	that is profitable	and sustainable?
Productivity Increases	N	Y	N
Quality Improvements	?	Y	N
Cost Reductions	N	Y	N
Sales Training	Y	Y	N
Mergers & Acquisitions	Y	?	N
Market-Facing Innovation	Y	Y	Y

BUSINESS BUILDERS

CHAPTER 6: BUILDERS PURSUE MARKET-FACING INNOVATION

be an initiative you turn on and off. Understanding and meeting market needs should define your company. This is what Builders do.

A CONSTANT TUG-OF-WAR

Market-facing innovation is far from easy. Builders understand they're in a never-ending tug-of-war between delivering differentiated and commoditized products. Differentiated

> "THE BUSINESS ENTERPRISE HAS TWO—AND ONLY TWO—BASIC FUNCTIONS: MARKETING AND INNOVATION. ALL THE REST ARE COSTS."
>
> —Peter Drucker

products provide value to customers they cannot get elsewhere, allowing the supplier to charge a premium price.

When you offer commoditized products, you compete on one thing. Price. Not only does this degrade your profit margins, it forces you to work with customers who have little loyalty to—or even respect for—your company. It's a particularly difficult tug-of-war because everyone outside your company is actively working against you:

- Purchasing agents try to make your products interchangeable with others.
- Competitors work hard to knock off your best products.
- New substituting technologies attempt to obsolete yours.
- New market entrants try to gain market share at your expense.
- Natural product life cycles play out over time.

COMMODITIZED PRODUCTS

DIFFERENTIATED PRODUCTS

- Purchasing agents
- Competitors' knock-offs
- Substituting technologies
- New market entrants
- Product life cycles

- New products that deliver more customer value than products from competitors

DIFFERENTIATION COMES FROM YOU, OR IT DOESN'T COME AT ALL.

Against all this you have only one defense: New products that deliver more customer value than competitors' products. It's sobering but true: differentiation comes from you, or it doesn't come at all.

THE COMMODITY DEATH SPIRAL

Product differentiation is hard work, but Builders know the alternative is worse. Consider the Commodity Death Spiral. Imagine a business stops innovating, leaving it with undifferentiated products that are interchangeable with competitors' products. This fact has not gone unnoticed by customers' purchasing agents, who demand lower pricing.

This means lower profits for the business, which is unfortunate because it's budgeting time, and the general manager's boss seems quite interested in next year's operating plan. Does the general manager say, "Sorry, boss, our profits are going down next year"? Probably not. Instead, the GM promises the same or higher profits, which means cost reductions are needed.

DOES THE GM SAY, "SORRY, BOSS, OUR PROFITS ARE GOING DOWN NEXT YEAR"?

Now the GM can't fire the salespeople. They're needed next year, so R&D and marketing budgets are cut. This means the business will have even less new product development capability next year, giving it even fewer options then. Eventually, the business reaches the point of no return where it can no longer recover. It goes out of business or is acquired for a pittance.

Not only has this business destroyed its capacity to thrive, it has destroyed its *will* to do so. If you were a Builder, would you stay in this business? Would you join it?

THE COMMODITY DEATH SPIRAL

This downward spiral begins when your business stops creating high-value, differentiated products. Purchasing agents notice your products are interchangeable with competitors' products, and they demand lower prices.

This reduces your profits. To avoid budgeting for lower profits next year, you cut costs. These are typically marketing, R&D, and any other costs that won't damage financial results in the near term.

Of course, this degrades your ability to create future differentiated products. Unless a Builder turns this around, your business eventually dies or goes onto "life support" where it's no longer relevant.

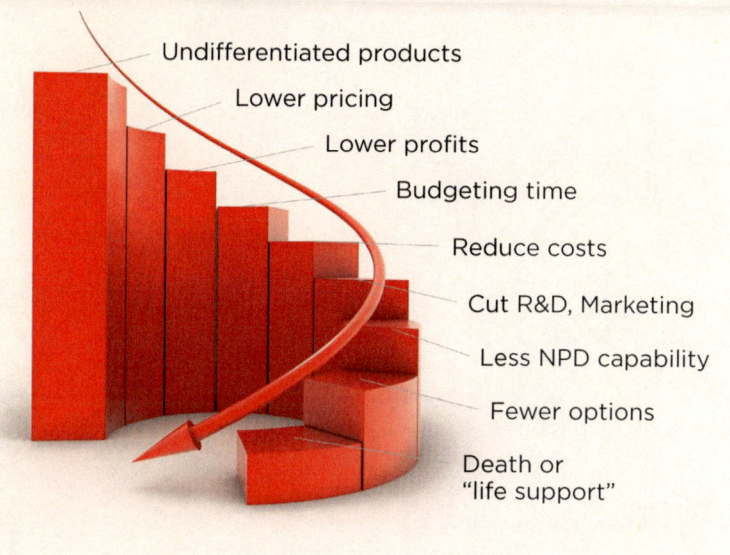

COMMODITY DEATH SPIRAL
- Undifferentiated products
- Lower pricing
- Lower profits
- Budgeting time
- Reduce costs
- Cut R&D, Marketing
- Less NPD capability
- Fewer options
- Death or "life support"

CHAPTER 6: BUILDERS PURSUE MARKET-FACING INNOVATION

Here's the antidote for this slow-motion train wreck: You need a Builder's steady passion for market-facing innovation. And you need to give your Builder enough time. Builders work on a very different time scale than Remodelers, Decorators, and Realtors, as you'll see in the next chapter. That's one reason they're successful.

JEAN ANGUS

Builders have an unrelenting passion for delivering innovative solutions to customers. Jean Angus, the recently retired president and CEO of Saint-Gobain Life Sciences, is a perfect example. During her senior leadership tenure, the business growth rate more than doubled, and already-impressive profits improved further. How? *Market-facing innovation.*

Originally a bench chemist, she became Director of Innovation Processes, guiding many businesses through workshops to understand their unique, core competencies, target the right markets, and gain skills to understand customer needs.

As Jean said, *"*If you do this in depth, you know which markets will reward your strengths and exactly which customer needs to address. Innovation then becomes obvious."

As president and CEO, Jean focused on creating an *enduring culture*. Jean gathered Net Promoter Scores from employees and customers to ensure year-over-year improvement. She created a common mission, "We create a better life," so *every* employee could contribute.

And she worked to get the right leaders in the right positions. Jean said, "The next leaders will have different strengths and will challenge the organization in different ways. But they need to fit culturally for the business to stay on a healthy growth trajectory."

CHAPTER 6: BUILDERS HAVE LONG TIME HORIZONS

CHAPTER 7
BUILDERS HAVE LONG TIME HORIZONS

> "Time is nature's way of keeping everything from happening at once."
>
> —JOHN ARCHIBALD WHEELER

CHAPTER 7: BUILDERS HAVE LONG TIME HORIZONS

Why is it difficult for companies to achieve profitable, sustainable growth? We've discussed several reasons:

- Leaders never learned the building trade on their way up.
- Leaders try to please shareholders more than other stakeholders.
- Leaders pursue personal career goals over business health.
- Leaders fixate on initiatives that don't drive reliable, long-term growth.

Regardless of the cause, there's one characteristic shared by all companies struggling with reliable growth: their time horizons are too short.

> **LEADERS' ACTIONS IN THE SHORT TERM *ALWAYS* IMPACT THE LONG TERM, AND USUALLY IN AN INVERSE AND AMPLIFIED FASHION.**

It's simply not possible to optimize for the short term and long term at the same time. Why? Leaders' actions in the short term *always* impact the long term, and usually in an inverse and amplified fashion. This is explained by first order and second order effects.

FIRST ORDER AND SECOND ORDER EFFECTS

In the early 1900s, the French colonial government of Hanoi faced an exploding rat population. So they placed a bounty on rat tails people turned in. The first order effect was lots of rat tails turned in. Good news, right?

But there were two second order effects. First, they noticed lots of tailless rats in the city, as residents favored amputation over extermination. Second, several rat-breeding farms were established.

ACTION:
- Put a bounty on rat tails

FIRST ORDER EFFECT:
- Many rat tails turned in

SECOND ORDER EFFECTS:
- Tailless rats
- Rat-breeding farms

Whenever you change a system to deliver a first order effect, you will always have a second order effect. If your first order effect was desirable, your second order effect will usually be undesirable. And vice versa.

The nineteenth century French economist Frédéric Bastiat put it this way: "It almost always happens that when the immediate consequence is favorable, the later consequences are disastrous, and vice versa. . . . Often, the sweeter the first fruit of a habit, the more bitter are its later fruits."

You see this every day. Enjoying unlimited jelly-filled donuts (first order effect) is more fun than ill-fitting clothes later (second order effect). Grinding through daily exercise (first order effect) is hard, but it lets you keep up with your grandkids (second order effect). Champion weightlifter and poet Jerzy Gregorek provided us with a simple formula: "Easy decisions, hard life. Hard decisions, easy life."

> YOU MAY *THINK* YOU'RE TIPPING JUST ONE DOMINO, BUT THERE'S *ALWAYS* A SECOND DOMINO THAT WILL TIP LATER.

When you take an action, you may *think* you're tipping just one domino, but there's *always* a second domino that will tip later. And usually more dominos after that.

BUSINESS BUILDERS

CHAPTER 7: BUILDERS HAVE LONG TIME HORIZONS

Consider how this applies to your business. You're nervous about the financial results for the coming quarter, so you freeze discretionary spending. Good news: You meet this quarter's earnings target. But your spending freeze also slowed dozens of new product projects as teams waited to run outside lab tests, hire technicians, interview customers, and so on.

FIRST DOMINO FIXATION

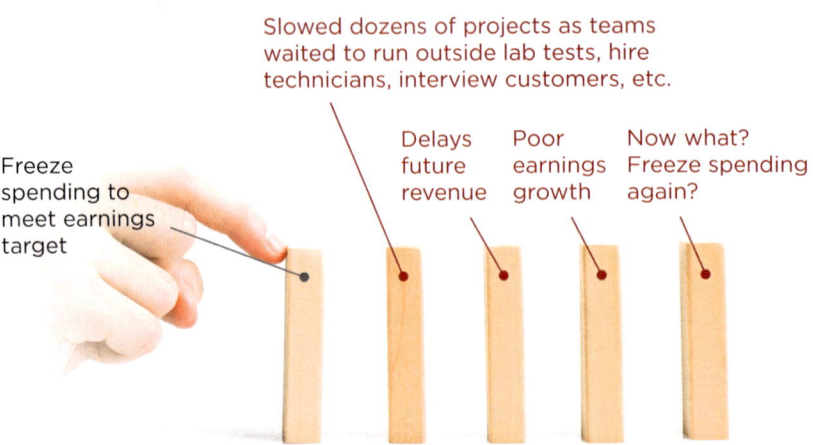

Product launches are pushed back as a result and this delays future revenue, leading to poor revenue and earnings growth. This is not the profitable, sustainable growth you had hoped for.

What do you do now? Freeze spending again? Business leaders are clever about many things, but they often suffer from *first domino fixation*. They're only thinking about that first domino.

Unfortunately, most business leaders don't learn from their experience. Ever sit through a financial review where the leadership team laments poor earnings growth? How often have you heard one of them say something like: *Well our problem today is all those crazy spending freezes the last few years?* Never?

I call this *first domino amnesia*. A short business time horizon works both ways: Leaders fail to look far enough into the future to *foresee* the impact of their decisions. And they fail to look far enough into the past to *understand* the cause of their problems. A lack of foresight and understanding can't be healthy.

FIRST DOMINO AMNESIA

Have you ever heard this in a financial review?

"Well, our problem is all those past spending freezes."

Poor earnings growth

FREQUENT COST CONTROLS

Near-term actions like spending freezes are a problem today. We asked survey respondents about the frequency of near-term cost controls (e.g., spending freezes, travel bans, hiring delays, and layoffs). Thirty-one percent of employees in companies growing faster than competitors said near-term cost controls are implemented too often. This climbs to 56 percent for companies growing slower than competitors.

Senior leaders agreed with their subordinates. In fact, somewhat *higher* percentages of senior leaders in both types of companies said these cost controls were too frequent. Just consider that: most employees at slower-growth companies believe near-term cost controls are being over-used, *and the leaders who called for them agree!*

BUSINESS BUILDERS

CHAPTER 7: BUILDERS HAVE LONG TIME HORIZONS

This leads to an obvious practical step for the Builder. There are many things "to do" if you want to be a renowned Builder. But you can start by *not* doing what others too often do: rely on near-term cost controls. Say no thanks to that jelly-filled donut.

Employees at one company told me they always try to get their meaningful work done in the first part of the year. That's because they know spending freezes will come as the year progresses. It's reasonable to expect a rainy season in Cambodia, but what does it say when employees can predict a business slow season their leaders arbitrarily impose?

> IT'S REASONABLE TO EXPECT A RAINY SEASON IN CAMBODIA, BUT WHAT DOES IT SAY WHEN EMPLOYEES CAN PREDICT A BUSINESS SLOW SEASON THEIR LEADERS ARBITRARILY IMPOSE?

A rainy season brings mud, which turns forward progress into a slow slog. Same with near-term cost controls. If an executive edict

SELF-IMPOSED GROWTH FRICTION TURNS MARKET-FACING INNOVATION INTO A *SLOG*.

Spending Freezes   Hiring Delays   Layoffs
     Travel Bans   Re-organizations
Rapid Job Changes   Shifting Strategies   New Initiatives

TOO MANY NEAR-TERM COST CONTROLS

About half of employees at faster-growth companies said near-term cost controls were implemented at about the right frequency. Still, nearly one-third said these occurred too often.

At slower-growth companies, fully 56 percent of employees said near-term cost controls were implemented too frequently.

Surprisingly, senior leaders were even a bit unhappier with cost controls than their subordinates.

HOW OFTEN DOES YOUR COMPANY IMPLEMENT NEAR-TERM COST CONTROLS (E.G., SPENDING FREEZES, TRAVEL BANS, HIRING DELAYS, LAYOFFS)?

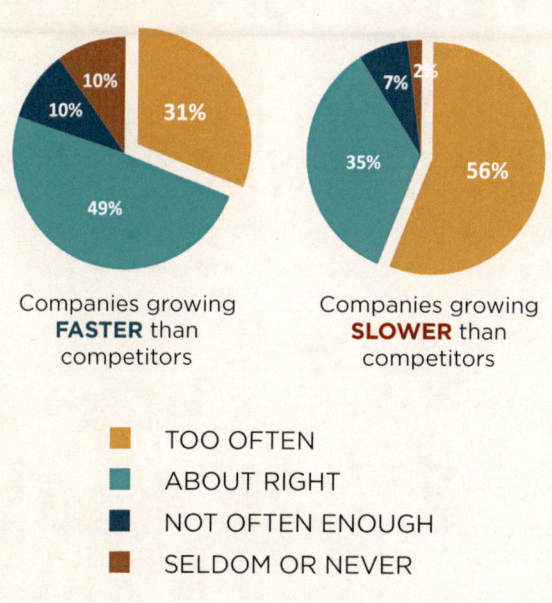

Companies growing **FASTER** than competitors

Companies growing **SLOWER** than competitors

- TOO OFTEN
- ABOUT RIGHT
- NOT OFTEN ENOUGH
- SELDOM OR NEVER

BUSINESS BUILDERS

is likely to slow market-facing innovation, leaders have introduced *growth friction*. This is a handicap on growth they've chosen to self-impose. The most obvious forms are near-term cost controls such as travel bans, spending freezes, hiring delays, and layoffs.

But growth friction also occurs when a restless leadership team makes any change too frequently. Rapid shifts in organizational structure, job responsibilities, company-wide initiatives, and strategy may be well-meant, but they're still disruptive.

In 1982, Dr. W. Edwards published his fourteen points for management, the first of which encouraged "constancy of purpose." This is what your new product teams need. Market-facing innovation works best when employees aren't nervously looking over their shoulders wondering, *what next?*

THE HARD TRUTH IS THAT SOME LEADERS COULD IMPROVE THEIR BUSINESS GROWTH BY STAYING HOME AND DOING NOTHING.

The hard truth is that some leaders could improve their business growth by staying home and doing nothing. Before taking an executive action, the business leader should think long term. Near-term cost controls may be appropriate at times, but senior leadership teams should understand and debate their second order effects before enacting them.

DOES LONG-TERM BEHAVIOR REALLY WORK?

A helpful study was published in *Harvard Business Review*. A study of 615 US companies over fourteen years showed those exhibiting long-term behavior had better financial results than those with short-term behavior. On average, the former group had 47 percent higher revenue, 36 percent higher earnings, 58 percent higher market capitalization, and 132 percent higher job creation.[25]

TIME ALLOCATION OF SENIOR LEADERS

In our survey, we asked how senior leaders allocated their attention to three time horizons: current year, next three years, and beyond three years.

We were surprised to see how accurately subordinates estimated their leaders' time allocation—to the nearest percentage point—compared to leaders' responses. Note to leaders: They're paying attention!

Senior leaders at companies growing slower than competitors allocated more time to the current year (47 percent) than leaders at faster-growth companies (38 percent).

Leaders at both companies spent a third of their time on the next three years, but faster-growth leaders spend more time thinking beyond three years (29 percent versus 21 percent for slower-growth companies).

HOW DO SENIOR LEADERS IN YOUR COMPANY ALLOCATE THEIR ATTENTION TO EACH OF THESE TIME HORIZONS?

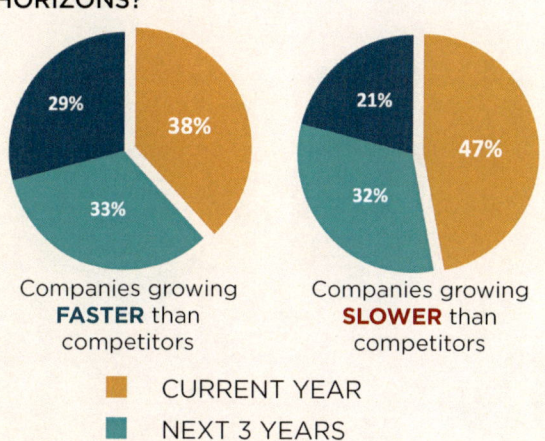

CHAPTER 7: BUILDERS HAVE LONG TIME HORIZONS

Shane Parrish said it well: "What looks like success is often just patience."

Is it difficult to move from a near-term time horizon to a longer one? It can be, but perhaps not as difficult as you imagine. Builders understand that investing in the future now can take several years for the payoff. Expect near-term results to suffer for a while as longer-term investments are made.

But Builders know this discomfort is only temporary. Once they cross this chasm of discomfort, they'll never need to do so again. If future investments continue unabated after the chasm, they achieve a flywheel effect, and this chasm need not be crossed again. (See sidebar based on our financial model.)[26]

PICK UP THE LONG LEVER OF TIME. THAT'S WHAT BUILDERS DO.

Builders know how to use levers. They know they can move much more with a long lever than a short one. When senior leaders focus their attention on the near term, they restrict themselves to a short lever that only moves small loads short distances. Pick up the long lever of time. That's what Builders do.

COMPANIES EXHIBITING LONG-TERM BEHAVIOR HAD:

47% Higher Revenue

36% Higher Earnings

58% Higher Market Cap

132% Higher Job Creation

CROSSING THE CHASM OF DISCOMFORT

What penalty do you pay for moving into a high-growth mode? In this financial model, a business with $100 million revenue increases spending on new product development in year two by 50 percent. It enjoys much higher revenue and EBITDA in later years. But at what cost in the near term?

Very little: The chart on the right shows a dip in EBITDA from 15 percent to 13 percent for a few years. After crossing this chasm, it need *never be crossed again*.

Ask your financial team to create a model for your business. Your chasm may not look too bad, especially if you only cross it once.

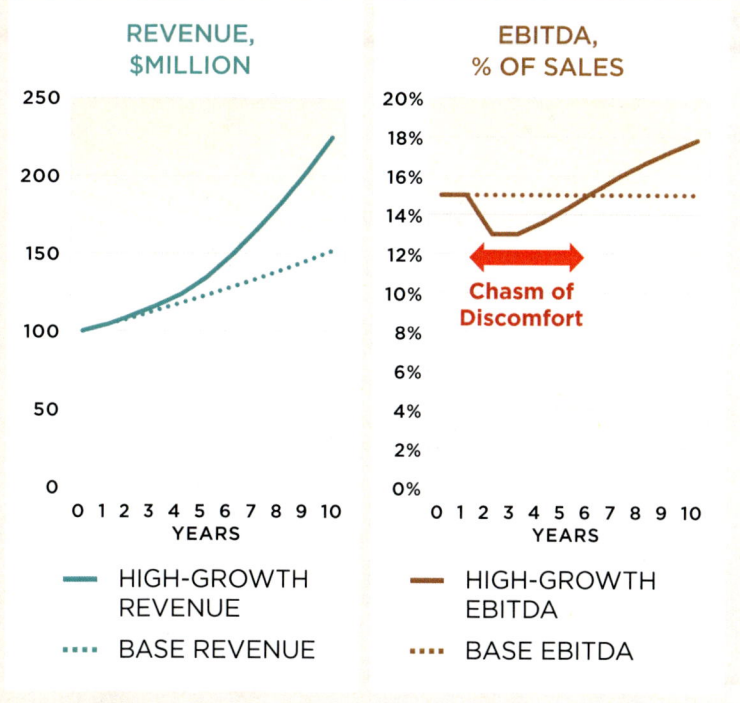

BUSINESS BUILDERS

SHOULD YOU ELIMINATE LAYOFFS?

I'd like to close this chapter with a challenge: Should your senior leadership team set a goal of eliminating layoffs except as a last resort? I've met strong Builders who have engaged in mass layoffs, so this isn't a blanket criticism of past actions.

But remember that layoffs used to be uncommon. In his book *The Disposable American*, Louis Uchitelle explains that prior to the 1970s, mass layoffs were rare and seen as "a sign of corporate failure and a violation of acceptable business behavior."[27]

The cost of mass layoffs is high, both to employees and the health of the business. Studies show that laid-off employees suffer 83 percent higher odds of a new health condition, twice the level of depression, four times the risk of substance abuse, and up to three times the risk of suicide.[28] And how many times have you heard of families torn apart geographically while one spouse keeps their existing job or the kids finish high school?

If your plan is to leave your business stronger than you found it, mass layoffs may be one of your most formidable roadblocks:

- One study found employees retained after a layoff experience a 20 percent drop in job performance and a 36 percent decline in organizational commitment.[29]
- Another study found the number of new inventions post-layoff fell by 24 percent.[30]
- Other research showed downsizing a workforce by just 1 percent leads to a 31 percent increase in voluntary turnover the next year.[31]

I've spoken to many employees going through downsizing, and I consistently see market-facing innovation stall out as employees shift their attention from the top of Maslow's Needs Hierarchy (self-actualization) to lower levels (security, food, shelter, etc.).

But could your senior leadership team realistically eliminate mass layoffs in all but the most dire situations? With good planning, I believe it could—perhaps not this year or the next—but eventually. Consider the common reasons for layoffs:

Placating shareholders: If you have long-term investors, they don't *want* you taking near-term actions that degrade your long-term prospects. In chapter 12, we'll explore ways to shift from a near-term to long-term investor base. Besides, you should consider all stakeholders, and it's your *employees* that will supercharge your Building program more than any other group.

> **LONG-TERM INVESTORS DON'T *WANT* YOU TAKING NEAR-TERM ACTIONS THAT DEGRADE YOUR LONG-TERM PROSPECTS.**

Economic cycles: Given the dozens of economic cycles since the mid-1800s, we should hardly be surprised by the next one. There's much you can do to plan for them and mitigate their impact:

- Instead of over-hiring in peak times, outsource and engage recent retirees to handle higher demand.
- Avoid high debt leverage, and instead build financial reserves.
- Use furloughs or temporary salary reductions as needed instead of permanent job loss.
- Use the downturn for training and other retooling so you can accelerate out of the recession.

Unfavorable trends: Some of your businesses will certainly face inescapable headwinds, so *diversify*. Make it your business to study the future, transforming your portfolio of businesses ahead of the curve. I once saw a letter from Thomas Jefferson to the DuPont company praising it for the explosives he bought from them to blow up his farm's tree stumps. So it's possible for a company to keep adapting over *centuries*.

CHAPTER 7: BUILDERS HAVE LONG TIME HORIZONS

Getting outcompeted: If you are truly on a strong Building program, this shouldn't happen, at least not for your business in aggregate. After all, our research shows there are plenty of Decorators, Remodelers, and Realtors leading companies today. With Builders in charge, you should be able to understand and meet customer needs better than such competitors.

I hope your leadership team will imagine a future without layoffs. Picture an experienced, dedicated workforce confidently innovating for customers. One that keeps building its shared knowledge and growth capabilities while competitors experience high turnover, massive retraining, and corporate amnesia.

William McKnight, an early 3M president, believed in the power of employees. He said, "If you put fences around people, you get sheep." I'd add that you certainly don't want nervous sheep worrying about their personal security. Instead, unleash the power of your employees' trust and loyalty and invite them to build something great with you.

YOU DON'T WANT NERVOUS SHEEP FOR EMPLOYEES.

CHAPTER 8
BUILDERS KNOW FINANCE IS A SPECTATOR SPORT

> "Informed decision-making comes from a long tradition of guessing and then blaming others for inadequate results."
>
> —SCOTT ADAMS

CHAPTER 8: BUILDERS KNOW FINANCE IS A SPECTATOR SPORT

I once worked for a CEO who was quite adept at financial reviews. It didn't matter how many spreadsheets he had to flip through, he would always zoom in on "the problem." We all hoped he'd find it in someone else's business, because the interrogation that followed was . . . unpleasant.

As we left one such review, he asked me what I thought of the meeting. I said it was OK, but it reminded me of my first job as a freshly minted chemical engineer, watching over an extruder on the midnight shift. Of course, I had to explain *that*.

My job was to watch the hot synthetic rubber being squeezed out of the end of the extruder exit die. I would take periodic samples and run several quality control tests. If the product quality coming out of the die was bad, did I stand there and exhort the die to do better? I did not. I checked what was going into the feed hopper.

That's because I could do absolutely nothing at the extruder exit die to improve the rubber. Perhaps I could make small adjustments in the temperature and screw speed inside the extruder, but invariably I needed to fix the raw material being fed *into* the extruder.

TO IMPROVE RESULTS, FOCUS ON THE FEED HOPPER, NOT THE EXIT DIE.

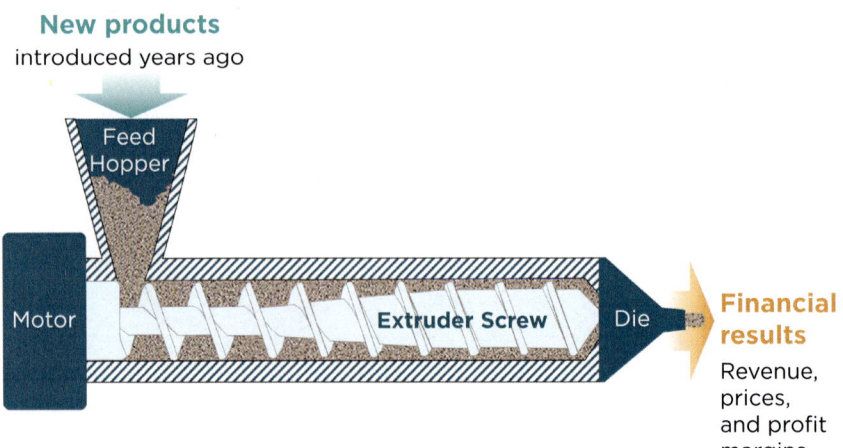

86

Our financial reviews were like the extruder exit die. Oh, they *seemed* intelligent, as we discussed revenue, prices, and profit margins. But all those financial results were predetermined by the new products we had fed into the machine years earlier.

> **ALL THOSE FINANCIAL RESULTS WERE PREDETERMINED BY THE NEW PRODUCTS WE HAD FED INTO THE MACHINE YEARS EARLIER.**

Same with your financial reviews. If you're not happy with the results you're reviewing at these meetings, it's because low-quality raw material was fed into your hopper years ago.

Want more gratifying financial reviews in a few years? The *only* way is to understand and meet customer needs better than others right now. You need to fill your new product pipeline with products customers love. Differentiated, high-value offerings they can't get elsewhere. Only by doing this will you see strong growth rates, higher prices, and better profit margins in your future financial reviews.

SPECTATOR VERSUS PARTICIPANT SPORT

Some leaders argue they need to take care of the near term so they can keep their jobs. That's true, but at some point you need to ask, *Do I want my career to be a spectator sport, or a participant sport?*

> **THERE'S NOTHING YOU CAN DO AT THE EXTRUDER EXIT DIE TO MAKE A *POSITIVE* CHANGE.**

When you're standing at the extruder exit die exhorting it to do better, you're a spectator. There's nothing you can do here to make a *positive* change.

But sadly, you can make *negative* changes at the extruder die. The overwhelming tendency during a financial review is to focus on surface problems, not root causes. To see why, consider introspection, impatience, and incentive:

- Introspection: understanding root causes requires unwelcome self-examination and mental effort.
- Impatience: few are looking for a solution that will take several years to pay off.
- Incentive: your accounting system measures and rewards actions leading to near-term results.

Most business leaders are simply not wired for inactivity. Faced with the choice between doing nothing at a financial review or "doing something," they'll choose the latter. Even if it's a bad idea. They'll find that first domino to push over and deal with those remaining dominos later.

MOST BUSINESS LEADERS ARE SIMPLY NOT WIRED FOR INACTIVITY.

As leaders try to upgrade current financial results, they often degrade the feed of new products needed for future financial results. They opt for travel bans, hiring delays, spending freezes, and layoffs. Such financial "fixes" are *precisely* what you'd do to put the brakes on future growth.

It's entirely possible for a business leader to sit through unending financial reviews and only see the financial results of their "braking" actions. Individual contributors have first-row seats to the real-world results:

- New product teams lack the time, resources, and skills to understand market needs.
- Understaffed, ill-equipped, and poorly aimed R&D fails to develop superior products.
- Engineers benchmark competitive products that have clear advantages over theirs.

- Sales reps are confronted by purchasing agents who have all the bargaining power.

This leads to disenfranchised employees, low morale, and a talent drain. It's the high-performing employees that leave first. They move to an organization that is relevant. One where they can make meaningful contributions. They move to an organization led by a Builder.

THESE FINANCIAL "FIXES" ARE PRECISELY WHAT YOU'D DO TO PUT THE BRAKES ON FUTURE GROWTH.

LAGGING VERSUS LEADING INDICATORS

Financial reviews focus almost exclusively on lagging indicators. You're discussing what has already happened. Running a business based on financial reviews is like driving a car by staring into the rearview mirror. When it comes to making fundamental, lasting improvements—not reactive cost controls—your review of financial results fails three tests:

1. **Not prescriptive:** It's difficult to understand the specific changes you need to make. Yes, you need higher-priced products, but does this require voice-of-customer training, new applications testing equipment, sales training, or something else?

2. **Not predictive:** You can't anticipate how your actions will impact future performance. Of all the meaningful actions you could take to boost profitable, sustainable growth, which will move the needle most for your business, and by how much?

3. **Not precise:** Your financial results are a complex aggregate of products, customers, and markets. Pursuing some of these will lead to a much greater financial reward than others. But you're unlikely to get this level of insight from financial reviews.

> **RUNNING A BUSINESS BASED ON FINANCIAL REVIEWS IS LIKE DRIVING A CAR BY STARING INTO THE REARVIEW MIRROR.**

For many leaders, their choices during financial reviews are to do nothing, or do something that makes future financial reviews even worse. Thankfully, there's a *tertium quid,* or third way. This is replacing many of those financial reviews with two other types of meetings.

The first is new product planning meetings, where you discuss the new products you're developing to delight your customers. Builder-leaders periodically review larger projects and engage in regular pipeline reviews of multiple projects. You're probably doing this today, but in later chapters we'll discuss ways to do it better.

The second is capability-building meetings to shape the competencies needed to deliver these products efficiently and effectively. This is dramatically underutilized at most companies, so we'll explore capability-building in the next chapter.

New product planning meetings are akin to the extruder feed hopper. The raw material you're adding is new products that will generate superior revenue, pricing, and margins in a few years.

Capability-building meetings are like upgrading the extruder machine itself. When you have well-trained, motivated teams working in a culture of innovation, you've got a powerful growth machine.

WHICH MEETINGS WILL CONSUME MOST OF YOUR TIME AND ENERGY?

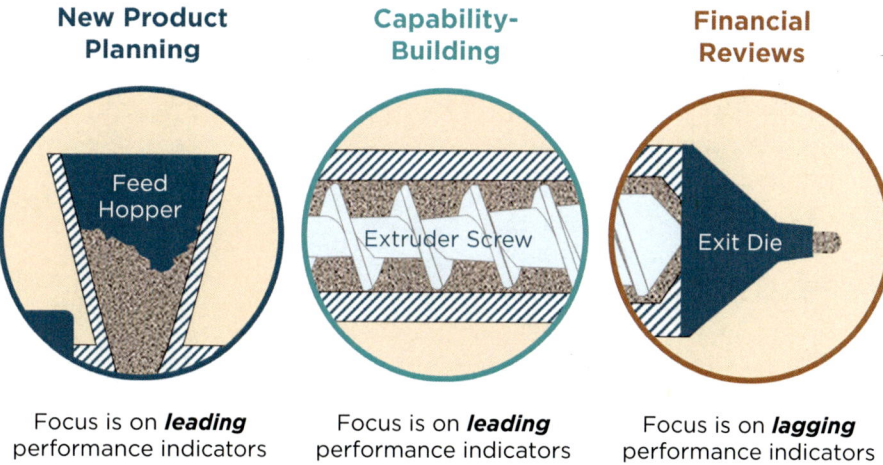

Both new product planning meetings and capability-building meetings revolve around *leading* indicators, not *lagging* ones. So where will your leadership team spend most of its time? You can't eliminate all financial reviews, but Builders keep them short and infrequent. They spend their time where it counts instead.

BUILDERS KEEP FINANCIAL REVIEWS SHORT AND INFREQUENT.

DECORATORS LOVE FINANCIAL REVIEWS, BUT ARE THEY OUT OF TOUCH?

Decorators love financial reviews. Our survey defined Decorators as senior leaders whose primary passion is presenting a favorable financial performance and outlook to investors. These reviews are important to them because they see financial results as their main "report card," not the longer-term building of their business.

We compared the views of individual contributors at Decorator-led and Builder-led companies. These respondents said Decorator leaders allocate 35 percent of their attention to presenting favorable financials, while Builder leaders devote only 18 percent of their attention to this same goal. Our survey also showed Decorators allocated more time to the current year, and employees at Decorator-led companies had lower growth expectations.

DECORATORS SEEM TO HAVE A DISTORTED VIEW OF REALITY.

These weren't surprising results, but *this* was unexpected: Decorators seem to have a distorted view of reality. When respondents were asked how fast their company was growing relative to competitors, we saw good agreement between the senior leaders and subordinates at Builder-led companies.

DO DECORATORS DELUDE THEMSELVES?

At Builder-led companies, there was good agreement between senior leaders and subordinates when they estimated their growth relative to competitors.

This was not the case for Decorator-led companies: 55 percent of senior leaders thought their company was growing faster than competitors, while only 33 percent of subordinates shared this view. Remodeler-led companies did no better: 52 percent of senior leaders and 27 percent of subordinates believed their growth was faster than competitors.

The subordinates probably got it right: With our large data set, it's unlikely over half of the companies were growing faster than competitors. It seems problematic if leaders misunderstand something as important as their relative growth.

QUESTION FOR DECORATOR-LED COMPANIES: HOW DOES YOUR GROWTH COMPARE TO COMPETITORS?

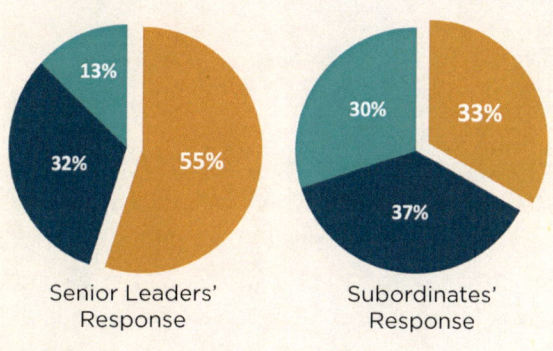

Senior Leaders' Response | Subordinates' Response

- GROWING FASTER
- GROWING SAME AS COMPETITORS
- GROWING SLOWER

This wasn't the case for Decorator-led companies. Fifty-five percent of Decorator-leaders felt they were growing faster than competitors, but only 33 percent of their subordinates agreed. They can't both be right. And given our large survey sample size, the subordinate pie chart—with equal thirds—seems more plausible. (See sidebar.)

Is this caused by senior leaders' limited understanding of the competition? Wishful thinking? An ingrained habit for "telling a good story?" We don't know, but if your senior leaders are fixated on financial results, there's a good chance they are

- devoting much of their energy to a spectator sport, not a participant sport.
- damaging longer-term growth when they "take action" by implementing near-term cost controls.
- deluding themselves into believing their business's growth is better than it really is.

In chapter 4, we saw this paradox: too much focus on shareholder wealth today can detract from the healthy growth needed for future shareholder wealth. We see the same paradox here: too much focus on financial results today can degrade future financial results.

Consider three reasons for this. First, the time and energy a Decorator devotes to today's financial results is time and energy that is not available for the Building trade. Second, the typical actions taken to "fix" near-term financials end up damaging longer-term business performance. Third, financially focused leaders may have a distorted view of reality. These conditions are not precursors to profitable, sustainable growth.

If you've decided to back off this spectator sport, what do you replace it with? Nature abhors a vacuum, after all. In the next chapter we'll suggest you focus on *building capabilities*.

MAKERS AND TAKERS

Do you see an intense focus on financial results in your company? You're not alone. Your company has been swept up with others in a larger macro trend.

In her book *Makers and Takers*, Rana Foroohar explains that finance used to work for business. Now business works for finance. Finance represents 7 percent of the American economy, while it takes 25 percent of corporate profits and creates only 4 percent of all jobs.[32]

Foroohar shows how Makers—those creating real value—have become servants of Takers who "enrich themselves rather than society at large."[33]

It's unlikely you'll change this macro trend. Just be sure you don't mirror it within your company.

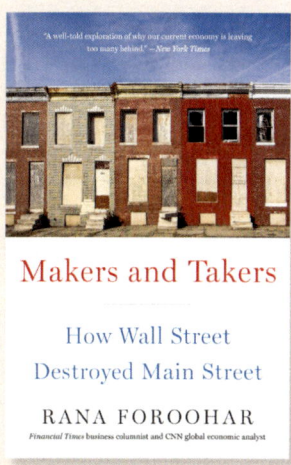

FINANCE USED TO WORK FOR BUSINESS.

NOW BUSINESS WORKS FOR FINANCE.

CHAPTER 8: BUILDERS KNOW FINANCE IS A SPECTATOR SPORT

CHAPTER 9
BUILDERS STRENGTHEN BUSINESS CAPABILITIES

> "Long-range planning does not deal with the future decisions, but with the future of present decisions."
>
> —PETER DRUCKER

CHAPTER 9: BUILDERS STRENGTHEN BUSINESS CAPABILITIES

What would happen if you went to your senior leaders and told them you think they're too focused on results? If you try this let me know how it works out. While it might not be a career-enhancing conversation, chances are you'd be right. Unless they're a Builder, most senior leaders are overfocused on *results* and underfocused on *capabilities*.

Imagine you've decided to climb El Capitan, but you've got the wrong footwear, you're out of shape, and you have no climbing skills whatsoever. In other words, you have no capabilities. Yes, that's true, you say, but you *really* want to climb El Capitan. You want *results*!

MOST SENIOR LEADERS ARE OVERFOCUSED ON RESULTS AND UNDERFOCUSED ON CAPABILITIES.

Unfortunately, some business leaders don't think much about capability-building. This ensures no long-term improvement. Their business is like the golfer stuck at the same handicap or the pole vaulter who never goes higher. They fixate on results this year, hit the reset button, and do it all over again next year, giving little thought to capabilities.

CAN YOU THINK OF ANY HUMAN ENDEAVOR WHERE CHAMPIONS DON'T FOCUS FIRST ON CAPABILITIES AND THEN RESULTS? OTHER THAN . . . UHMM . . . BUSINESS?

WHICH IS *YOUR* MAIN QUADRANT?

The notion of capability-building isn't new. In *The 7 Habits of Highly Effective People*, Stephen Covey encouraged a balance between P (production) and PC (production capability).[34] P is the golden egg, while PC is the goose. P is split firewood, while PC is the sharpened axe. For our purposes, P is financial results, while PC is any capability needed to drive those results.

The capabilities your business needs for strong financial results could include voice-of-customer skills, R&D know-how, competitive testing, patent protection, talent management, a culture of innovation, or something else.

In chapter 7 we talked about time horizons, specifically near term versus long term. Let's add the element of time to our exploration of results versus capabilities. Considering results versus capabilities and the near term versus the long term, senior leaders can devote their attention to any of four quadrants:

- **Quadrant 1. Near-term results:** This is the Decorator's domain, where a good deal of financial reviewing and reporting takes place. But there is little reliable long-term

BUILDERS DRIVE RELIABLE GROWTH BY BOOSTING LONG-TERM CAPABILITIES.

BUSINESS BUILDERS

99

growth that occurs. As the saying goes, *lots of dirt was flyin,' but not many holes were dug*.

- **Quadrant 2. Long-term results:** An example is a long-term incentive plan, which *can* provide helpful motivation. Some think this checks the box for dealing with the long term, but it doesn't. Like all desired results, it's insufficient unless the proper capabilities are built to drive those results.

- **Quadrant 3. Near-term capabilities:** Remodelers work here, implementing sales force training, productivity improvements, etc. These can be quite helpful, but we classify them as near term because they don't lead to *sustainable* long-term growth, as explained in chapter 6.

- **Quadrant 4. Long-term capabilities:** This is the domain of Builders. They don't build just *any* capabilities. They focus on those needed to boost market-facing innovation. This is what your company's founder(s) did, and it remains the only path to profitable growth that is *sustainable*.

ARE WE OUT OF BALANCE TODAY?

We wanted to understand how senior leaders strike a balance between Quadrant 1 (near-term results) and Quadrant 4 (long-term capabilities). To do this, our survey asked subordinates how their senior leaders balanced these two.

The results were not encouraging: nearly half of all subordinates (47 percent) said senior leaders were too focused on near-term results, while only 11 percent felt leaders were too focused on long-term capabilities. As you might guess, results were the worst at Decorator-led companies, with 58 percent of subordinates citing imbalance toward near-term results.

> **NEARLY HALF OF ALL SUBORDINATES (47 PERCENT) SAID SENIOR LEADERS WERE TOO FOCUSED ON NEAR-TERM RESULTS.**

OUT OF BALANCE

We asked subordinates if their senior leaders were too focused on near-term results, too focused on long-term capabilities, or had the proper balance between the two.

Within companies growing faster than competitors, 29 percent said their leaders were too focused on delivering near-term results. For companies growing slower, this number grew to 72 percent. In all our research, the greatest differentiator between faster- and slower-growing companies was this leadership balance between near-term results and long-term capabilities.

As with all our research, this shows correlation and does not prove causation. But it seems companies desiring faster growth would do well to tamp down their fixation on near-term results and focus more on building capabilities for future growth.

SUBORDINATES: HOW DO YOUR SENIOR LEADERS BALANCE NEAR-TERM RESULTS AND LONG-TERM CAPABILITIES?

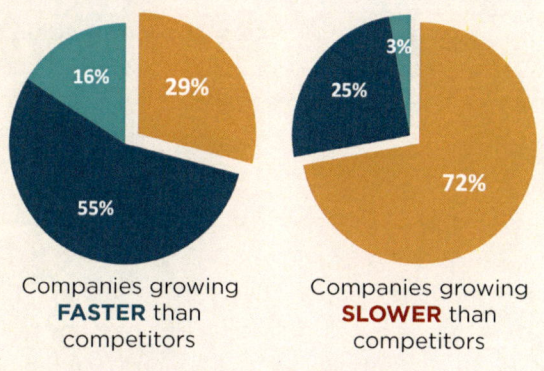

Companies growing **FASTER** than competitors: 29% / 55% / 16%

Companies growing **SLOWER** than competitors: 72% / 25% / 3%

- TOO FOCUSED ON NEAR-TERM *RESULTS*
- PROPER BALANCE
- TOO FOCUSED ON LONG-TERM *CAPABILITIES*

BUSINESS BUILDERS

We also found a correlation between this balance and reported growth rates. Within companies growing faster than competitors, 29 percent said their leaders were too focused on delivering near-term results. Within companies growing slower than competitors, this number grew to an alarming 72 percent. (See sidebar.) Two other points are worth noting:

1. **Unhappy senior leaders:** While senior leaders weren't as displeased as subordinates with their imbalance, they were far from satisfied. In slower-growth companies, fully 57 percent of senior leaders said they were too focused on Quadrant 1, near-term results.

2. **No "overkill" on long-term capabilities:** We could find *no* cases where most of the respondents thought the balance had shifted too far into Quadrant 4, long-term capabilities. This was true even for Builder-led companies and companies growing faster than competitors.

We find the last point interesting. Even our survey's subset of Builder-led companies may not represent the best possible balance; for every subordinate in a Builder-led company that complained about too much long-term capability-building, *four* subordinates complained about too much focus on short-term results. There's probably upside potential for even today's Builder-led companies to improve their capability-building.

WHAT CAPABILITIES SHOULD YOU BUILD?

In Quadrant 4, long-term capabilities, *long term* doesn't just indicate how many years will pass before a company realizes the benefits of its capability-building. It also infers that the benefits are *sustainable*. In other words, once the capability is in place, it will continue to generate benefits for a long time.

This capability is typically something that allows the company to understand and meet customer needs better than others. It might be employee training in voice-of-customer methods or perhaps technology leadership. By sustainable, I don't mean the capability lasts forever. Apple Computer couldn't stop competitors from copying its edge-to-edge phone displays. But this technological capability gave them years of competitive advantage and a platform for adding more capabilities.

Many fine initiatives (e.g., quality and productivity improvements) do not meet this standard because they reach a point of diminishing returns.

For this reason, all Quadrant 4 capabilities necessarily support growth from market-facing innovation. As explained in chapter 6, market-facing innovation is the only way to drive profitable, *sustainable* growth. You may remember that you'll only achieve this reliable growth if you *understand and meet customer needs better than others do*.

YOU'LL ONLY ACHIEVE THIS RELIABLE GROWTH IF YOU UNDERSTAND AND MEET CUSTOMER NEEDS BETTER THAN OTHERS.

We could have simply said *meet* customer needs, but we didn't because so many companies struggle with the first step of *understanding* customer needs. We'll explore how Builders understand customer needs in the next chapter. Incorporating both *understanding* and *meeting* customer needs gives us a useful framework to organize Quadrant 4 capabilities.

In the following diagram, twenty-four market-facing innovation capabilities are classified into helping a company

- understand customer needs,
- meet customer needs, or
- both understand and meet customer needs.

CHAPTER 9: BUILDERS STRENGTHEN BUSINESS CAPABILITIES

This is just one way to organize your Quadrant 4 capabilities. It's important to collect all possible capabilities first, and then plan which you'll pursue most aggressively. Your list will depend on your business and industry. (We'll provide some guidance for B2B companies in Appendices A and B.)

BUT HOW DO YOU MEASURE PROGRESS?

As you shift your balance from near-term results to long-term capabilities, you'll face a dilemma: How do you measure progress? Imagine you're the CEO and want to ensure your division vice presidents are building long-term capabilities, not just manipulating near-term results until they can jump to their next job. You want them to be "Bills," not "Cals."

Your financial accounting system doesn't "account" for this, so who can tell you the straight story? Subordinates can. Conduct confidential capabilities surveys annually with all employees to determine if key capabilities in each group or division are being strengthened or weakened over time.

> YOUR FINANCIAL ACCOUNTING SYSTEM DOESN'T "ACCOUNT" FOR CAPABILITY-BUILDING, SO WHO CAN TELL YOU THE STRAIGHT STORY?

You might have a division VP who is "managing up" quite nicely and posting great near-term financials, all while destroying the division's growth capabilities. The employees in this division know what's going on. And it bothers them. Your survey is a type of 360-degree evaluation that serves as a counterbalance to the near-term pressure for "results" that all executives face.

In the next sidebar you'll see an example of such a diagnostic we've created for B2B companies, using the twenty-four market-facing capabilities cited earlier. This example provides two types of benchmarking:

1. **Peer-based benchmarking:** In this case, data was collected on many companies, allowing the diagnosed business to compare its current capabilities with other companies.
2. **Time-based benchmarking:** This diagnostic is typically repeated annually to see if a business is progressing, regressing, or remaining static on important growth capabilities.

Don't worry if you lack access to a peer database to understand your relative capabilities. It's more important to measure how you're progressing over time. Consider this three-step process:

1. Engage your employees to assemble a complete list of capabilities that could help you drive growth through market-facing innovation.

2. As part of your strategic planning process, create a road map to build the most critical capabilities over several years.
3. Survey your employees annually to gauge the progress you're making on these capabilities.

Is this overkill? Probably not. You've seen that many senior leaders are overly focused on the near term, and there's nothing in your accounting system to counteract this. Unless you establish a *capability* accounting system to counterbalance your *results* accounting system, change is unlikely to occur.

> **UNLESS YOU ESTABLISH A *CAPABILITY* ACCOUNTING SYSTEM TO COUNTERBALANCE YOUR *RESULTS* ACCOUNTING SYSTEM, CHANGE IS UNLIKELY TO OCCUR.**

What capabilities are Builders especially strong in? They are *very* good at understanding the needs of their customers. In the next chapter we'll see why this is so.

"ACCOUNTING SYSTEM" FOR CAPABILITIES

Here's one example for measuring progress in capability-building. (For details, visit www.b2bgrowthdiagnostic.com.)

All market-facing employees are asked to evaluate their business's current capabilities in twenty-four areas. Descriptors are provided for numerical ratings to ensure a consistent interpretation of each.

This database includes data from other companies. But more important than peer-based benchmarking, is time-based benchmarking. Employees should be asked to complete this survey annually.

This accountability encourages business leaders to build capabilities for the long term, not just generate near-term results.

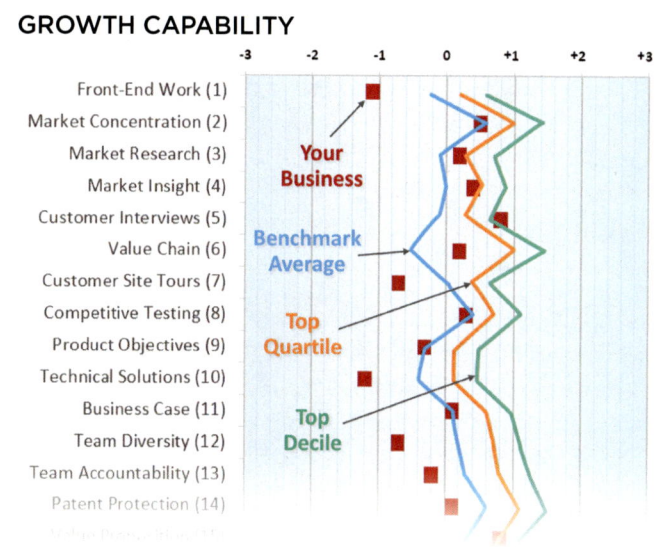

BUSINESS BUILDERS 107

KEES VERHAAR

Builders have difficulty suppressing their make-it-better gene, even in tough times. Kees Verhaar joined Arizona Chemical as its president in September 2008, and *immediately* faced the uncertainty of a painful recession. His decision? Start building.

Over the next several years, he astonished observers with his capability-building. One remarked, "I've never seen anyone who trains this much, Kees!"

Scores of marketing, technical and sales staff were trained in advanced voice-of-customer interviewing methods. One market-facing project after another was launched. Entire new markets were developed, and the business was transformed into a growth machine.

Less obvious but highly potent were the "soft" changes: 360-degree performance reviews, emotional intelligence training, and encouraging a culture of risk-taking. Kees reflected, "I would take the blame when things went wrong, so they'd see it was OK to fail as long as we learned from it."

Over the next five years, this billion-dollar business grew by more than 30 percent, while EBITDA margins increased from 10 percent to more than 20 percent. Beyond financial success, employees felt the thrill of personally making a difference, as they learned "the building trade."

CHAPTER 10
BUILDERS UNDERSTAND CUSTOMER NEEDS

> "If we have data, let's use it. If we have opinions, let's use mine."
>
> —JIM BARKSDALE

CHAPTER 10: BUILDERS UNDERSTAND CUSTOMER NEEDS

Let's step back and check the logic flow that brought us to this chapter:

- Instead of fixating on shareholder wealth, your company should meet the needs of *all* stakeholders.
- To meet the needs of all stakeholders, your primary goal should be profitable, sustainable growth.
- The only way to achieve profitable, *sustainable* growth is through market-facing innovation.
- Successful market-facing innovation comes from understanding and meeting customer needs better than others.

In this chapter, we'll focus on the *understanding* part of understanding and meeting customer needs. When developing a new product or service, companies move through three phases:

1. **Design:** Often called the front end of innovation, this leads to a proposed design for the new product. If customers' needs are not well understood, there's a high *commercial risk* of failure.

THREE PHASES OF MARKET-FACING INNOVATION

1. Design

2. Development

3. Launch

Commercial risk is addressed here

Technical risk is addressed here

110

2. **Development:** Next, chemists, engineers, software developers, and others try to create a new product that meets the design criteria. If they fail to meet the criteria, it's due to *technical risk*.

3. **Launch:** Finally, the product is launched, with marketing and sales working in tandem to build revenue.

It's possible that your company is great at *understanding* customer needs—the design phase—and must improve meeting customer needs in the development and launch phases. But you'd be an outlier. Research shows most companies will benefit more by improving how they *understand* customer needs.

> RESEARCH SHOWS MOST COMPANIES WILL BENEFIT MORE BY IMPROVING HOW THEY *UNDERSTAND* CUSTOMER NEEDS.

WHAT THE RESEARCH SHOWS

In addition to our survey on leadership, we conducted another survey to better understand what drives profitable, sustainable growth.[35] As part of our survey, 540 respondents evaluated twenty-four growth drivers. They said the most important driver of growth was "delivering offerings with strong, differentiated value propositions." In other words, successful market-facing innovation.

We then compared responses from companies that claimed to be good at delivering strong value propositions to those that said they did a poor job. We wanted to know which behaviors differentiated these two groups. The three greatest differentiators between the strong and weak providers of value propositions (in order) were:

1. **Front-end work:** Conducting pre-development work to understand market dynamics, customer needs, and competition before significant investment.

2. **Market concentration:** Concentrating innovation resources on key market segments that are winnable and worth winning.
3. **Customer interviews:** Conducting interviews to uncover, understand, and prioritize customers' important, unmet needs.

All three of these address *understanding* customer needs. Drivers associated with *meeting* customer needs—such as technical solutions, patent protection, gate review process, and new product launch—showed less differentiation between strong and weak providers of value propositions.

Another vantage point is to ask what causes most new product failures. Research conducted in 1971 revealed the major cause to be "inadequate market analysis."[36] This problem has persisted for five decades, with "no market demand" cited as the leading root cause of new product failures in a 2021 study.[37] (See next sidebar.)

> **INNOVATION MOST OFTEN FAILS DUE TO A POOR UNDERSTANDING OF CUSTOMER NEEDS.**

This problem appears in startups as well. After "running out of cash" (39 percent), the leading cause of startup failures in 2021 was "no market need" (35 percent), which was well ahead of the next one, "got outcompeted" (20 percent).[38] The common theme? Innovation most often fails due to a poor understanding of customer needs.

There's one more reason for companies to focus more on *understanding* than *meeting* customer needs. It's easier and cheaper. If you want your R&D to do a better job at *meeting* customer needs, what will you do? Hire scientists that are 20 percent brighter than competitors? Hire more R&D staff? Hire the next Steve Jobs?

In contrast, most companies can do a much better job at

understanding customer needs without spending a fortune. (This is especially true for B2B companies, a point we'll explore in Appendix A.) Your success in understanding customer needs begins with a new mindset.

RETHINKING CUSTOMER NEEDS

You'll do a better job understanding customer needs when you use precise language to describe the following three-step sequence:

1. **Market segment:** This is the *cluster of customers with similar needs* that will be the target of your innovation efforts. In the example below, you might target manufacturers of passenger cars.
2. **Customer job to be done:** Define the task or objective you hope to improve for customers in this market segment. In this example, you'll help auto designers and engineers build a better dashboard in passenger cars.

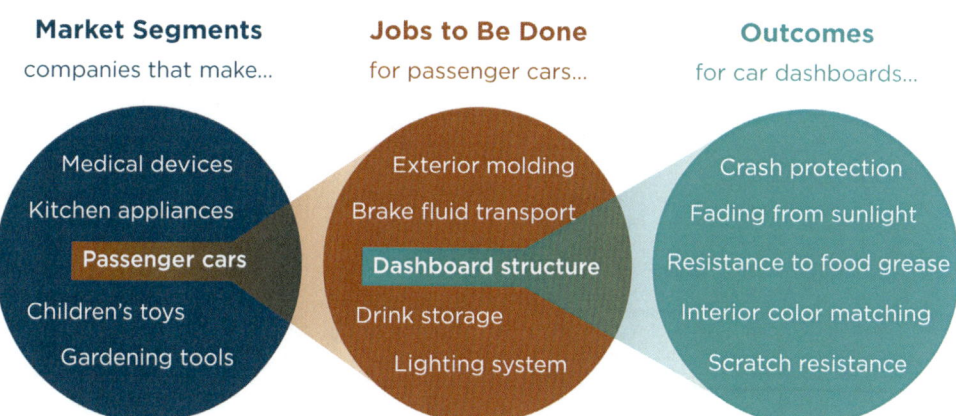

HOW TO FOCUS YOUR INNOVATION IF YOU MAKE PLASTIC COMPONENTS

Market Segments — companies that make...
- Medical devices
- Kitchen appliances
- **Passenger cars**
- Children's toys
- Gardening tools

Jobs to Be Done — for passenger cars...
- Exterior molding
- Brake fluid transport
- **Dashboard structure**
- Drink storage
- Lighting system

Outcomes — for car dashboards...
- Crash protection
- Fading from sunlight
- Resistance to food grease
- Interior color matching
- Scratch resistance

BUSINESS BUILDERS

CHAPTER 10: BUILDERS UNDERSTAND CUSTOMER NEEDS

MISUNDERSTANDING CUSTOMER NEEDS... FOR FIVE DECADES

When it comes to market-facing innovation, most companies struggle to properly understand the needs of their target customers. As a result, they invent "cures for no known diseases."

This was first documented in 1971, with the leading cause of new product failures found to be "inadequate market analysis." A 2021 study found the leading root cause to be "no market demand."

Your objective in market-facing innovation should be to understand and meet customer needs better than others. Most companies will do well to improve their capabilities in the *understand* part.

1971
Contributing causes of failure

Inadequate market analysis	**45%**
Product problems or defects	29%
Lack of focused marketing effort	25%
Higher costs than anticipated	19%
Competitive strength or reaction	17%
Poor timing of introduction	14%
All other sources	36%

2021
Major cause of failure

No market demand	**42%**
Poor performance	32%
Insufficient complementary assets	16%
Poorly defendable position	5%
Regulatory restrictions	5%
Total	100%

3. **Customer outcomes:** Finally, uncover and prioritize the desired end-results that customers want improved within their job to be done. These outcomes might include improved crash protection, better resistance to french fry grease, less fading from sunlight, etc.

MARKET SEGMENTS

A market segment is a cluster of customers with similar needs, and it's usually the best target for your innovation efforts. Some companies are *customer-reactive*, trying to please one customer at a time. Most would be more successful by being *market-proactive* instead.

> MOST COMPANIES WOULD BE MORE SUCCESSFUL IF THEY WERE *MARKET-PROACTIVE* INSTEAD OF *CUSTOMER-REACTIVE*.

To understand why, consider two extremes. In the first case, the business leader says, "Let's sell a single product to all our customers so we can maximize efficiency." Examples of this one-size-fits-all model include commodities, such as a single grade of diesel fuel or one purity level of salt.

In the second case, the leader says, "Let's create a unique product for every one of our customers so we can maximize effectiveness." Examples of the custom shop approach include producers of private-label foods or customized prototypes.

Most businesses lie between these extreme endpoints, and business leaders must address the tension between maximizing efficiency (one-size-fits-all) and effectiveness (custom shop) in market-facing innovation.

What's the best way of resolving this tension? In most cases, you do this by innovating for one *market segment* at a time.

WHY INNOVATE FOR *MARKET SEGMENTS*?

← More EFFICIENT | More EFFECTIVE →

One-Size-Fits-All
One product for
ALL CUSTOMERS
Efficient but ineffective

Market-Focused
One product for
EACH MARKET SEGMENT
Best efficiency without losing effectiveness

Custom Shop
One product for
EACH CUSTOMER
Effective but inefficient

When you innovate for one market segment at a time, you sacrifice no effectiveness. Remember, our definition of a market segment is a cluster of customers with *similar needs*. Unlike the one-size-fits-all approach, your new product won't sub-optimize effectiveness by trying to please customers with *different needs*.

When your innovation is market-focused, you've lost no more efficiency than what's needed to maintain maximum effectiveness. Not so with the custom shop approach, where you develop multiple products when a single product would have sufficed.

Does this mean you should never develop a product for a single customer? No, some B2B customers are so large that such work is justified. Others may only divulge their needs on an exclusive basis, perhaps under a joint development agreement.

But you should *always* ask yourself if you'd be better off focusing on a market segment instead of a single customer. In the long run, optimizing effectiveness and efficiency provides a strong competitive advantage.

JOBS TO BE DONE

The late Clayton Christensen popularized the concept of jobs to be done.[39] He explained that when we buy a product, we essentially "hire" it to help us do a job. This is consistent with Theodore Levitt's famous declaration, "People don't want to buy a quarter-inch drill. They want a quarter-inch hole."

My friend and colleague Scott Burleson wrote a wonderful book on jobs to be done called *The Statue in the Stone*.[40] The title was inspired by Michelangelo's unveiling of the statue of *David*. When the pope asked how he created something so perfect from a block of marble, he apparently replied, "I removed everything that was not David."

Scott believes innovation shouldn't be thought of as *additive*, where new features are piled on. Instead, it's a matter of removing everything—like chunks of marble—that prevents perfection in the customers' job to be done.

"PEOPLE DON'T WANT TO BUY A QUARTER-INCH DRILL. THEY WANT A QUARTER-INCH HOLE."
—Theodore Levitt

Jobs to be done (customer task)

You can only improve a Job by improving its Outcomes

Outcomes (desired end results)
- Minimize time to drill
- Minimize effort to drill
- Minimize seizing
- Minimize splintering
- Minimize burn marks
- Minimize bore roughness

Solution (our product)

The outcomes we listed for drilling a hole are all about *removing* something that's preventing perfection: the time it takes, the effort it takes, and so on. Also notice these outcomes may be related to the customer's *process* (time, effort, seizing) or their final *product* (splintering, burn marks, roughness).

I've had the pleasure of coaching hundreds of new product teams in the front end of innovation and here's what I've found: The most successful teams focus on the customer's job to be done and its related outcomes. The less successful ones are fixated on their drill bit's metal hardness, alloy composition, and cutting edge.

CUSTOMER OUTCOMES

Tony Ulwick made a major contribution to the field of innovation with his focus on customer "outcomes."[41] He understood that using the word *needs* can be a confusing way to describe what innovators are trying to satisfy on behalf of customers. An outcome is a specific and measurable end-result the customer desires, such as minimizing the time it takes to drill a hole.

There are typically dozens and dozens of outcomes for every customer job to be done. I believe innovators should have two objectives in the front end of innovation:

1. **Uncover all relevant outcomes.** You must do this to eliminate *errors of omission.* This is failing to uncover a key outcome that could have led to an exciting new product. New product teams are never faulted for errors of omission at the time, because no one noticed what they missed.

2. **Prioritize customer outcomes.** Not all outcomes are equally relevant: Customers will only pay a premium if you improve an outcome that is both *important* and currently *unsatisfied*. When you identify these, you eliminate *errors of commission*. This is choosing the wrong outcomes to satisfy.

Imagine your company makes hydraulic cylinders for garbage trucks. A full set of relevant customer outcomes might include quieter operation, greater power, longer cylinder life, smoother operation at low temperatures, faster replacement time, and dozens more. But perhaps the only *high-priority* outcomes customers are eager for you to improve are longer life, greater power, and quieter operation. Shouldn't you learn this?

A popular way to uncover and prioritize outcomes is with voice-of-customer interviews. You should do these in two sequential rounds of interviews. First, conduct divergent, qualitative interviews to gather all customer outcomes. You typically *diverge* by asking the customer questions such as *Can you think of any other problems you encounter?*

Then conduct a second round of interviews, this time convergent and quantitative. Why quantitative? The language of math avoids confirmation bias, where you hear what you want to hear . . . and customers tell you what they think you want to hear. You collect importance and satisfaction ratings on a scale of one to ten for each outcome during the interviews.

First round of interviews is
QUALITATIVE

Second round of interviews is
QUANTITATIVE

You DIVERGE

to uncover all outcomes in the job to be done

You CONVERGE

to prioritize important, unsatisfied outcomes

BUSINESS BUILDERS

These direct-from-the-customer numerical ratings let you converge on customers' highest priorities: those which customers have rated as both important and currently unsatisfied. This approach is unbiased, unfiltered, and critical to your success.

These two types of interviews are especially potent when interviewing B2B customers. We explore them in more detail in Appendix B. For a five-minute demonstration video, visit www.VOCforB2B.com.

THE PROBLEM WITH PREMATURE SOLUTIONS

Did you notice we've said *nothing* so far about your new product or service? There's a time to show customers your prototypes, concept drawings, and samples. It's later.

When you're in the design phase—the front end of innovation—you should focus exclusively on your target market segment, job to be done, and outcomes. In other words, focus on reducing commercial risk in the design phase, and *then* deal with technical risk in the development phase.

A common error is to use the front end to study *both* commercial and technical feasibility at the same time. At first glance, this parallel work seems to make sense. A great way to go faster, right? But it reveals a "blurring" of the lines between product development and technology development.

Recall from chapter 6 that technology development is science-facing and turns money into knowledge. It builds company-wide capabilities that could be used in *multiple* markets. Product development is market-facing and turns knowledge back into money. Product development should focus on the needs of a *single* market segment.

If someone plans to do laboratory development work in parallel with customer interviews, a helpful question is, Will you be doing technology development or product development? If it's the former, allow it. If they say it's product development, your response should be, Why would you work on a solution to satisfy a market's needs before you know what those needs are?

WHY WOULD YOU WORK ON A SOLUTION TO SATISFY A MARKET'S NEEDS BEFORE YOU KNOW WHAT THOSE NEEDS ARE?

Consider three levels of innovation maturity: solution push, solution validation, and market insight.

1. Solution push occurs when a company starts with its own ideas of what they think or hope customers want. Then they develop a new product solution to meet these *imagined* needs. Crazy? You bet. But in some industries—especially B2B—this happens all the time.

THREE INNOVATION MATURITY LEVELS

3. MARKET INSIGHT — Start with *customer* outcomes. Develop solutions to these.

Here, you understand market **needs**.

Here, you only understand market **reaction**.

2. SOLUTION VALIDATION — Start with *your* ideas. Validate these with customers.

1. SOLUTION PUSH — Start with *your* ideas. Develop solutions to these.

Not sure this is happening? Ask someone for their company's diagram that explains their new product development process. There's a good chance the first stage is "idea generation," perhaps

BUSINESS BUILDERS

CHAPTER 10: BUILDERS UNDERSTAND CUSTOMER NEEDS

with a light bulb icon. Ask if this idea is usually theirs or their customers.' In my experience, it's usually the supplier's idea.

Future innovators will cringe when they look back at this. They'll find it hard to believe that companies went through the entire new product development process and *then* monitored new product sales to see if they got it right. Sure, this is one way to assess market needs. But can you think of a way to understand market needs that is *less* efficient than this? I cannot.

SOLUTION PUSH: IT'S HARD TO IMAGINE A MORE *INEFFICIENT* WAY TO UNDERSTAND MARKET NEEDS.

2. Solution validation is the next innovation maturity level. Once again, the company starts with its own ideas of market needs and develops solutions for these imagined needs.

Level 2 differs from Level 1 in that the supplier meets with customers to "validate" their solution: "You *do* like my great idea, don't you?" This is probably better than Level 1, but suffers from several deficiencies:

- **No diverging:** It's unlikely suppliers will hear any customer outcomes other than the handful their own solution addresses.
- **Highly biased:** Confirmation bias is seeking and interpreting information in a manner that confirms preconceived notions. It runs rampant with this approach.
- **No engagement:** Does your market have important customers you'd like to impress? This approach turns them off. They'd prefer a supplier who is interested in *their* needs, not the *supplier's* own ideas.

Solution validation is dangerous because practitioners think they are doing proper voice-of-customer work. But instead of understanding market needs, they're understanding market *reaction*—to one idea—their idea. These interviews usually seek customers' *approval* more than customers' *voice*. A common customer reaction is, "I'll bet their boss said they needed to get customer validation of their idea."

> INSTEAD OF UNDERSTANDING MARKET *NEEDS*, THEY'RE UNDERSTANDING MARKET *REACTION*—TO ONE IDEA—THEIR IDEA.

3. Market insight is the highest innovation level. Here you start with customers' desired outcomes. You complete a round of qualitative, divergent interviews, followed by a round of quantitative, convergent interviews. (We'll explore these in Appendix B.) As you'll see in the next section, this allows you to build a Certainty Time Machine for resolving commercial risk.

CERTAINTY TIME MACHINE

Market-facing innovation usually comes down to two primary forms of risk: commercial risk and technical risk. Your commercial risk is failing to understand which outcomes customers want improved, how much they want them improved, and how much they'll pay for these improvements.

Imagine you've resolved your commercial risk and have a product design that will satisfy customers. Your technical risk is failing to meet these design objectives. Remember our three new product development stages: design, development, and launch? The purpose of the development stage is for your scientists, engineers, and software developers to resolve technical risk.

When do you resolve commercial risk? You *could* wait until you launch your product to reach commercial certainty. This is what many companies do. Perhaps you've heard a conversation like this:

- Isabella: "How's your new product coming, Joe?"
- Joe: "Hard to say yet, Isabella. But we'll launch it next month and see if they buy it."

It's better to build a Certainty Time Machine. Instead of resolving commercial risk in the launch phase, resolve it months or years *earlier* in the design stage. If you conduct proper qualitative and

BUILD A CERTAINTY TIME MACHINE TO RESOLVE COMMERCIAL RISK EARLY

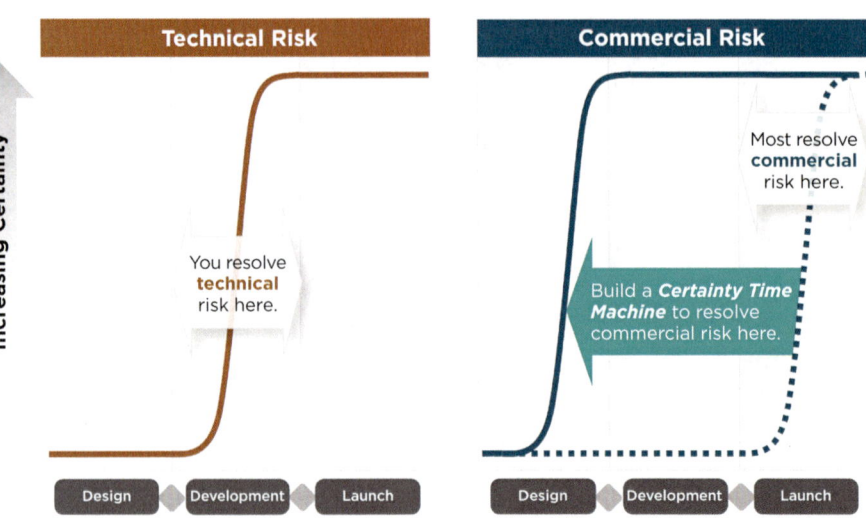

quantitative interviews, you'll learn everything you need to know about customer needs before the development stage begins.

Does this work for every market? No, but it does for B2B markets, and for consumer goods markets where consumers have adequate knowledge, interest, objectivity, and foresight. (See Appendix A for more.)

Just imagine your new product success rate if the *only* thing your developers had to worry about was technical risk. What if they *knew* customers would eagerly buy the new product so long as developers met the design criteria?

This may be the most practical Builder practice you can implement: stop allowing any substantial work in the development stage without divergent qualitative and (especially) convergent quantitative customer interviews.

CHAPTER 10: BUILDERS UNDERSTAND CUSTOMER NEEDS

CHAPTER 11
DOES THIS APPLY TO OUR BUSINESS?

> "Change-making happens when people fall in love with a different version of the future."
>
> —SETH GODIN

CHAPTER 11: DOES THIS APPLY TO OUR BUSINESS?

We've shared some unflattering data on leadership behavior across many companies, and you might wonder if your situation is different. After all, our research covered a broad range of companies with different

- ownership structure (public versus private)
- region (headquarter location)
- offerings (products versus services)
- markets (B2B versus B2C)
- size (annual revenue)

Your situation may indeed be different, especially if your leadership team has intentionally taken a different path. However, in general we didn't see major differences depending on the *type* of company. One exception is the size of your company. Spoiler alert: It's not good news for very large companies.

OWNERSHIP STRUCTURE (PUBLIC VERSUS PRIVATE)

We expected to see more long-term thinking at privately held companies than publicly traded companies. After all, these senior leaders shouldn't feel as obligated to satisfy share handlers on a quarterly basis. We were disappointed, as we saw only small differences between the two types of companies.

The following responses were logged from subordinates working in publicly traded companies (n = 360) and privately held companies (n = 142).

Senior leaders at privately held companies were *barely* more focused on Building, organic growth, and market-facing innovation. And they were nearly as inclined to implement near-term cost controls with a short time horizon.

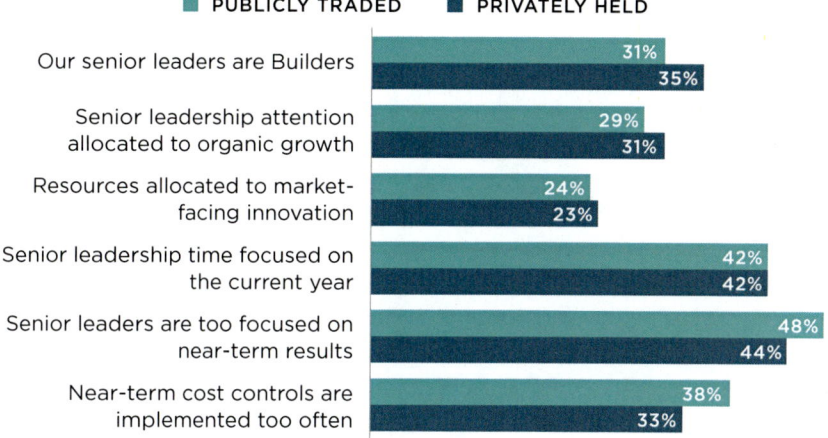

It's hard to understand why more leaders at privately held companies—free from Wall Street pressures—aren't engaged in the Building trade. Perhaps privately held companies have been hiring leaders from publicly traded companies, and old habits die hard.

It also might be that senior leaders at privately held companies have a communication problem. The above responses were from subordinates, while the chart below also shows responses from senior leaders. Note the large disparity at privately held companies between the percentage of Builders as estimated by subordinates (35 percent) versus senior leaders (68 percent).

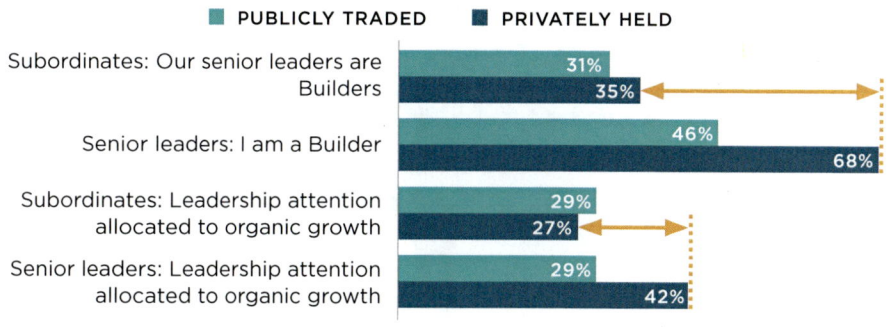

BUSINESS BUILDERS

CHAPTER 11: DOES THIS APPLY TO OUR BUSINESS?

Let's not rush to attribute this huge disparity to delusion on the part of senior leaders. Senior leaders at privately held companies also said they devoted 42 percent of their attention to organic growth, while their subordinates estimated this at only 27 percent. Could it be that these leaders' attention to organic growth isn't being recognized?

If you are a senior leader at a privately held company, consider how you are communicating—or failing to communicate—your true passion. It could be that your near-term cost controls and financial reviews are *masking* your passion for growth.

REGION (HEADQUARTER LOCATION)

Do leadership patterns change depending on which region your company is headquartered in? Not much. We had sufficient data for companies headquartered in North America (n = 449) and Europe (n = 145), and for limited analysis in Asia (n = 50). As shown below, responses from all job levels were generally similar for each of these three regions.

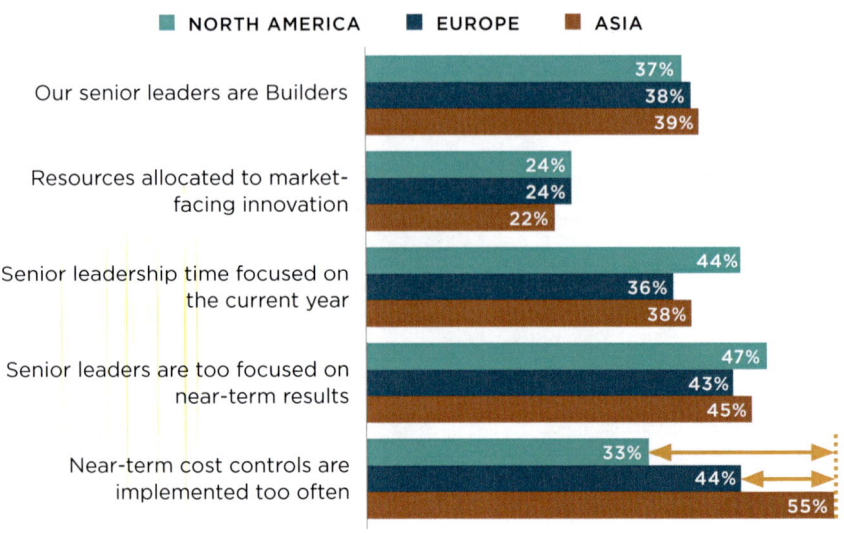

130

The greatest disparity was in the use of near-term cost controls. These were more frequently cited as being overused in Asia (55 percent) than in Europe (44 percent) or North America (33 percent). But we don't know if these cost controls were truly *used* more in Asia, or just *perceived* as being used too much.

It was interesting to see how subordinates versus senior leaders answered this question on overusing near-term cost controls across the regions:

- In Asia, they agreed with senior leaders at 57 percent and subordinates at 54 percent.
- In Europe, senior leaders were unhappier at 61 percent compared to subordinates at 38 percent.
- In North America, subordinates were unhappier at 35 percent compared to senior leaders at 26 percent.

You can expect to hear more complaining about these cost controls from European senior leaders (61 percent) than their North American counterparts (26 percent). But we don't know why. Beyond these views of near-term cost controls, though, it doesn't seem to matter much where your company is headquartered.

OFFERINGS (PRODUCTS VERSUS SERVICES)

We had more responses from producers of physical products than services. And because some of the service providers were small consultants, we trimmed the following data set to only include companies with revenue over $50 million.

The following chart shows the results for all job levels at these companies that offer physical products (n = 467) and services (n = 63).

CHAPTER 11: DOES THIS APPLY TO OUR BUSINESS?

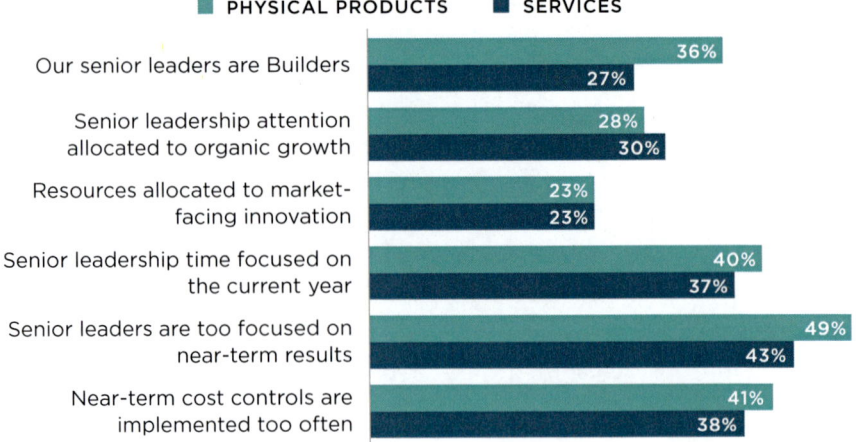

Since the data set for physical product producers was so large, the above results closely match the data you've seen in earlier chapters. What if your company provides services? You might have a slightly lower percentage of Builders, but this might just be data "noise." Overall, there doesn't seem to be any cause for service providers to change the impressions they've reached so far while reading this book.

MARKETS (B2B VERSUS B2C)

We received more responses from B2B companies selling to other businesses (n =550), compared to B2C companies selling directly to end-consumers (n = 96). The next chart shows the results for all job levels at B2B and B2C companies.

Given the large data set for B2B companies, these results closely match what you've seen in earlier chapters. If you hail from a B2C company, there's not much that's different here. One small exception: The focus on the near term at B2C companies isn't as great—or at least dissatisfaction with this focus—as in B2B companies. Overall, though, leaders seem to behave similarly in B2B and B2C companies.

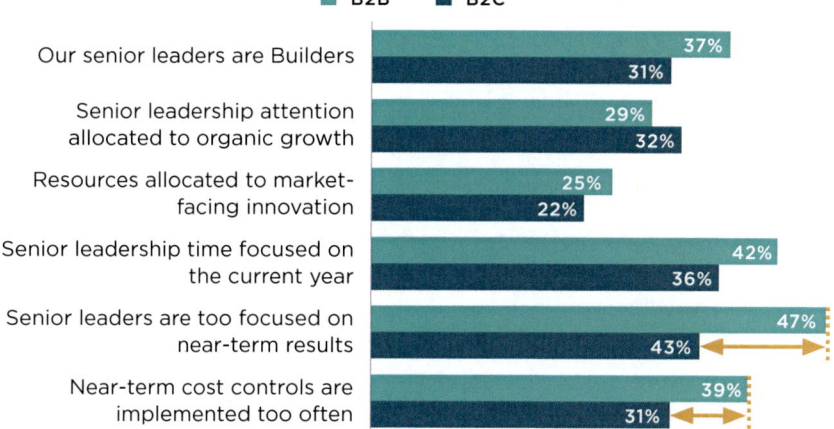

SIZE (ANNUAL REVENUE)

The story's been somewhat boring so far—not many differences in companies based on ownership structure, region, offerings, or markets. But company size—as measured by annual revenue—is different. In some cases, the differences were quite large.

We studied five different sizes of company, from annual revenue less than $50 million to over $5 billion. We had enough data to

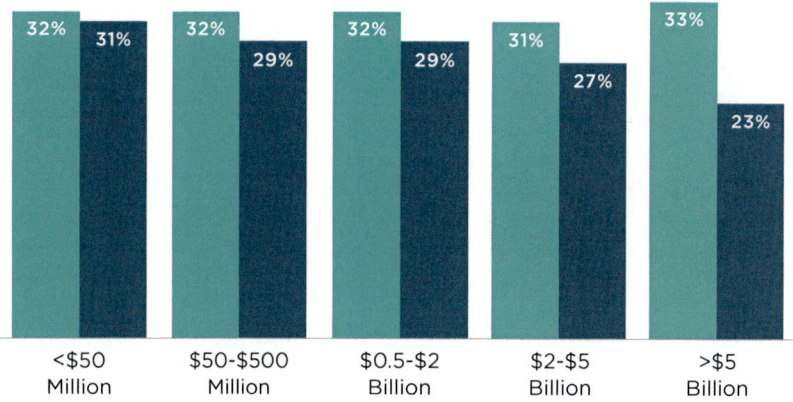

BUSINESS BUILDERS

examine just subordinate responses from each grouping (n = 88, 168, 110, 55, and 79, ordered from smallest annual revenue to largest).

We'll begin by looking at senior leaders' approach to organic growth. Regardless of company size, subordinates identified only about one-third of senior leaders as Builders. But as company size increased, subordinates saw less leadership attention allocated to organic growth.

We also compared senior leaders' responses with subordinates' responses and had a surprise with the largest companies. While only 33 percent of subordinates at these companies identified their leaders as Builders, 88 percent of these leaders thought of themselves as Builders! If you are a senior leader at a $5+ billion company, your employees probably see something different than what you see in the mirror.

Next, we looked at subordinates' views on the time horizons of senior leaders. Beginning with the second group ($50–$500 million), as the company size increased, senior leaders were thought to focus more on the current year. And with increasing size, these leaders were thought to spend less time in the three-plus year time frame.

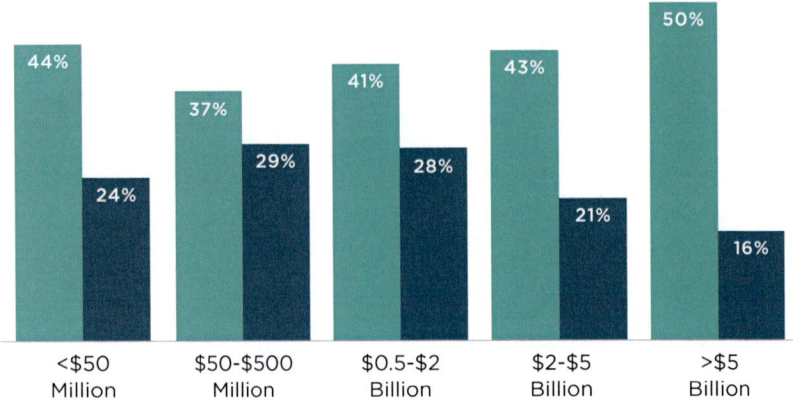

In general, senior leaders agreed with these estimates by subordinates. But for the largest companies (>$5 billion), senior leaders begged to differ; instead of spending only 16 percent of their time thinking about three-plus years, they claimed to spend 30 percent of their time here. Once again, there's a discrepancy between the self-image of very-large-company senior leaders and their subordinates' views.

For the two preceding charts, subordinates were asked to *estimate* senior leaders' behavior—their primary passion, their focus on growth, and their time horizons. In the next chart, subordinates were asked to *judge* senior leaders' behavior. They were asked if they were *too focused* on near-term results and if they implemented cost controls *too much*.

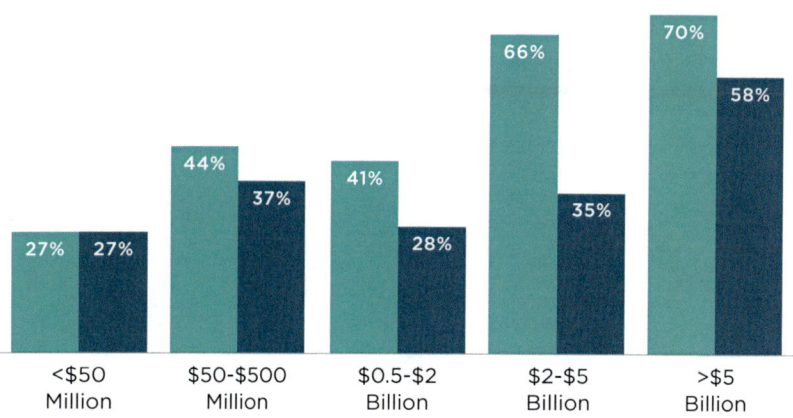

The above chart provides an alarming perspective for larger companies. For companies with revenue above $2 billion, about two-thirds of subordinates believe senior leaders are too focused on near-term results.

The balance between near-term results and long-term capabilities is displayed in the next sidebar. Whatever the reason, it can't

CHAPTER 11: DOES THIS APPLY TO OUR BUSINESS?

IMBALANCE AT LARGE COMPANIES

We asked subordinates about senior leaders' balance between near-term results and long-term capabilities. This balance was decent for the smallest companies.

But subordinates reported severe imbalance at larger companies. For companies with revenue over $2 billion, about two-thirds of subordinates said leaders were too focused on the near term.

If you're a senior leader at a large company, don't be surprised if most of your employees grumble about your next travel ban or discretionary spending freeze. They may also question your commitment to the future, given what they see as your meager building of long-term capabilities.

HOW DO YOUR SENIOR LEADERS BALANCE NEAR-TERM RESULTS AND LONG-TERM CAPABILITIES?

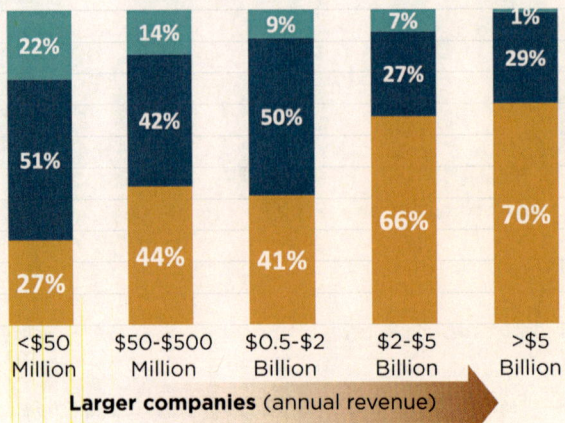

Revenue	Too focused on long-term capabilities	Proper balance	Too focused on near-term results
<$50 Million	22%	51%	27%
$50–$500 Million	14%	42%	44%
$0.5–$2 Billion	9%	50%	41%
$2–$5 Billion	7%	27%	66%
>$5 Billion	1%	29%	70%

Larger companies (annual revenue) →

- TOO FOCUSED ON LONG-TERM CAPABILITIES
- PROPER BALANCE
- TOO FOCUSED ON **NEAR-TERM RESULTS**

be good news that rank-and-file employees have such a disappointing view of their leaders' behavior.

IMPLICATIONS

These data lead to three implications. First, there's really no class of company that has escaped the leadership problems we've been discussing. It's not as though European companies have enough Builders, or privately held companies have long time horizons, or medium-size companies use cost controls sparingly, or service providers are great at market-facing innovation. The problems are pervasive.

Second, if you're a senior leader at a very large company, you may have extra work to do. It's likely your company's size, hierarchal levels, and perhaps momentum or complacency have moved your company further from the Builder ideals of your founders. Of course, your size can give you other advantages, so this is a matter of opportunity, not despair.

IT MATTERS LESS WHAT YOUR COMPANY *DOES* THAN HOW YOUR LEADERS *LEAD*.

Third and most important, it matters less what your company *does* than how your leaders *lead*. You've already seen data throughout this book revealing some companies that *are* led by Builders, that focus on long-term capabilities, that limit near-term cost controls, and that outpace competitors' growth. Firmographics don't explain these behaviors. Leadership does.

This is very good news. It's not easy to change the class of products you produce or the size of your company. Thankfully, you don't need to. You need to put Builders in charge and create the right environment for them to succeed. We'll see how in the next chapter.

CHAPTER 11: DOES THIS APPLY TO OUR BUSINESS?

CHAPTER 12
HOW DO WE CHANGE OUR BUSINESS?

> "Somebody needs to do something. It's just incredibly pathetic that it has to be us."
>
> —JERRY GARCIA

BUSINESS BUILDERS

It's clear that many companies are limiting their growth with unforced leadership errors, often from a loss of their founders' original Builder spirit. It's less clear how many will take the necessary steps to change their trajectory.

If your company is serious about making this change, it must start at the top of the organization. Consider implementing a three-step plan:

1. Put Builders in charge.
2. Create a Growth Capabilities Road Map.
3. Attract new investors.

1. PUT BUILDERS IN CHARGE.

Don't fire those who can improve operational efficiency, make acquisitions, or help you look good on Wall Street. You need them, but you need them in *supporting* roles.

You need Builders in leadership roles, and you need them soon. When you leave a Decorator in charge, you're failing to inspire employees and you're chasing away future Builders. You're also jeopardizing the rest of this three-part plan.

> **WHEN YOU LEAVE A DECORATOR IN CHARGE, YOU'RE FAILING TO INSPIRE EMPLOYEES AND YOU'RE CHASING AWAY FUTURE BUILDERS.**

How do you know if someone is a Builder? They have market-facing innovation in their DNA, a desire to build skills and capabilities, and a passion to make things better. And frankly, they aren't satisfied doing much else. You'll learn more looking at candidates' long-term career passion than their latest financial results.

You can't afford to hesitate with changes at the senior leadership level, but you can take more time with middle management. Give them a chance to show what they can do. Establish new measures of success, starting with their "duty" to leave their business stronger than they found it. Ask them for evidence that they're strengthening their business's long-term growth capabilities and have them explain their plan to do more of this.

When promoting a middle manager, it's easy to judge them based primarily on their financial performance. But it's a mistake. Remember Cal the Climber and Bill the Builder? Much of Cal's financial success came from his *predecessor's* hard work and his own short-term financial engineering. Bill's best work may not produce fruit until later, but if you're looking for long-term growth, promote Bill.

Not sure if senior leaders make that much difference? Most subordinates believe they do. In companies growing faster than competitors, 56 percent of them said senior leaders had "significant" or "the greatest" impact on organic growth. Senior leaders were perceived to have less impact at slower-growth companies. (See next sidebar.)

2. CREATE A GROWTH CAPABILITIES ROAD MAP.

Are you already in the habit of creating and updating a strategic plan? This could become your plan's most important component. Building the long-term capabilities to become a growth powerhouse doesn't take place in a single year. Nor does it make sense to bounce from one initiative to another in a haphazard fashion. You need a road map that is intelligently formed, embraced by the full leadership team, and communicated clearly and often to all employees.

Begin by developing a list of capabilities your company needs for strong organic growth driven by market-facing innovation. The possibilities vary depending on your type of business.

CHAPTER 12: HOW DO WE CHANGE OUR BUSINESS?

EXAMPLES OF GROWTH CAPABILITIES TO BUILD

- Customer interviewing skills
- Competitive insights
- R&D capabilities
- Transformational innovation
- Patent protection
- New product launch skills
- Gated project review process
- Project portfolio management
- Talent management
- Culture of innovation

Want strong employee buy-in to your road map? Conduct an employee survey measuring your business's current capabilities. For each listed capability, ask for an importance rating and a satisfaction rating. Place a high priority on improving capabilities with high importance scores and low satisfaction scores.

PLACE A HIGH PRIORITY ON IMPROVING CAPABILITIES WITH HIGH IMPORTANCE SCORES AND LOW SATISFACTION SCORES.

Next, put together a plan to boost those capabilities most likely to impact your growth. For B2B companies, for instance, there's evidence that improving the ability to *understand* customer needs (e.g., through voice-of-customer interviews) helps more than *meeting* customer needs (e.g., hiring more R&D staff).[42]

Over the decades, many companies have refined the way they *meet* customer needs. They do this with substantial R&D investment, gated product development processes, intellectual property protection, etc.

But our research shows many lag in their ability to understand and prioritize *which* needs to pursue. In other words, they're like archers that can shoot well, but don't know where to aim.

Plan to conduct an employee survey annually, and for large companies, do so within each group or division. Year-to-year trends will reveal which business leaders are building growth capabilities, and which are eating the seed corn needed for the business's future.

Publish your Growth Capabilities Map and your survey results for all employees to see. Make it clear that your goal is to understand and meet customer needs better than others. With clarity, transparency, and consistency on your part, you'll find you get a lot of inspired help.

3. ATTRACT NEW INVESTORS.

If yours is a publicly traded company, you need patient investors who, like you, are focused on the longer term. If your quarterly earnings take a dip while you stay focused on the future, these investors will understand. In fact, they don't *want* you making poor first-domino decisions that damage your long-term growth.

THESE INVESTORS DON'T *WANT* YOU MAKING POOR FIRST-DOMINO DECISIONS THAT DAMAGE YOUR LONG-TERM GROWTH.

When you meet with investors, try to assess if they're in this for the long haul *with you*. If you recommended this book, would they keep it on their nightstand . . . or rip out the pages to line the bottom of their birdcage?

Too many company leaders make the excuse, "We'd like to focus on the future, but investors won't let us." That argument doesn't hold up. In Amazon's early years, Jeff Bezos led the company through seven years without showing a profit. Far from penalizing Amazon, Wall Street cheered it on. Its leader had communicated a vision of growth, and this is what you must do.

CHAPTER 12: HOW DO WE CHANGE OUR BUSINESS?

Reintroducing your company to investors in this fashion doesn't need to be your first step. After all, you won't incur a financial hit for putting Builders in place or creating a Growth Capabilities Road Map. These are no-cost steps, so you don't need to gain investor support for them.

"COMPANIES OBTAIN THE SHAREHOLDER CONSTITUENCY THAT THEY SEEK AND DESERVE."

—Warren Buffett

When *do* you begin sending signals to long-term investors? Do it too soon and it might seem like you've got a story without substance. Do it too late and your stock will be punished when you make the right decisions judged by the wrong investors.

We suggest sharing elements of your Growth Capabilities Road Map when you can do so buoyed by early successes. Examples of market-facing innovation that led to positive financial results will be well received.

I've seen billion-dollar businesses completely reinvent themselves in this manner. It's not easy and it takes several years. But as a leader, you won't be on your own. You'll have many highly-motivated employees coming alongside to join you.

LEADERSHIP IMPACT ON GROWTH

We asked subordinates how much their senior leaders' behavior impacted the company's organic growth. At companies growing faster than competitors, 56 percent said leaders had "significant" or "the greatest" impact.

We saw different results at companies growing slower than competitors. Here the "significant or greatest" impact dropped to 37 percent.

Not all "impact" by company leaders is necessarily positive. Some respondents may have felt their leaders' overuse of cost controls indeed impacted growth, but in a negative fashion. Regardless, leaders make a difference.

HOW MUCH DOES SENIOR LEADERSHIP BEHAVIOR IMPACT YOUR COMPANY'S ORGANIC GROWTH? (AT FASTER-GROWTH COMPANIES)

- NO IMPACT
- SOME IMPACT
- MODERATE IMPACT
- SIGNIFICANT IMPACT
- GREATEST IMPACT

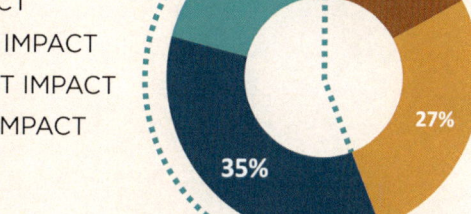

BUSINESS BUILDERS 145

CHAPTER 12: HOW DO WE CHANGE OUR BUSINESS?

CHAPTER 13

HOW DO I BECOME A BUILDER?

> "Trying and struggling looks like incompetence right up until the moment it looks like success."
>
> —SHANE PARRISH

CHAPTER 13: HOW DO I BECOME A BUILDER?

Perhaps you have no desire to become a business leader. That's perfectly understandable—I've met many chemists, engineers, sales professionals, and others who have enjoyed fulfilling careers without any leadership responsibilities.

If you don't want to become a leader yourself, try to join an organization led by a Builder. You'll have three benefits compared to working for a Decorator. First, you'll have more job security. There's no guarantee against layoffs at a Builder-led company, but they are far less frequent than at Decorator-led companies.

> **IF YOU DON'T WANT TO BECOME A LEADER YOURSELF, TRY TO JOIN AN ORGANIZATION LED BY A BUILDER.**

Second, you'll avoid a great deal of frustration. Within Decorator-led companies, you keep experiencing the growth friction discussed in chapter 7. Just when you're about to make meaningful progress, you're hamstrung with travel bans, spending freezes, and hiring delays.

Third, you get to work with top-notch colleagues in a Builder-led organization. Builders hire, train, and promote other Builders. Decorators chase away would-be Builders and promote people like Cal the Climber. With whom would you prefer to spend forty to fifty hours per week?

What if you do want to be a business leader recognized, admired, and trusted as a Builder? It depends on your starting point: individual contributor, middle manager, or senior leader.

STARTING POINT FOR INDIVIDUAL CONTRIBUTORS

Builders start by building themselves. They build their *experience* and their *skills*.

Load up on experience in market-facing innovation, also known as new product or service development. If you're currently in a marketing, product management, or technical role, this will be a natural fit for you. Become an integral part of new product development teams from start to finish: front end, development, and launch.

What if you're in a different role today—perhaps sales, operations, supply chain, finance, or something else? The best new product teams are multifunctional. They need your help.

- Sales professionals can set up and attend voice-of-customer interviews.
- Operations can plan for the eventual production of the new offering.
- Supply chain can address customer concerns as well as plan for the new offering.
- Finance can build value calculators and make financial projections for the new offering.

THE BEST NEW PRODUCT TEAMS ARE MULTIFUNCTIONAL.

THEY NEED YOUR HELP.

Make yourself essential to the success of your team, and future teams will seek you out. You'll find yourself spending more and more time gaining experience in market-facing innovation.

What about skills? It's amazing how adept someone can become at anything with a dedicated approach over time. Many just need to replace some TV time with learning time, and then consistently practice what they've learned. Here are just a few examples:

- **Creating slide presentations:** In *Multimedia Learning*, Richard Mayer presents fifteen principles for combining words and graphics. He shows how these principles—based on over two hundred experiments—improve both comprehension and retention.
- **Developing business strategy:** For me, the classic on developing business strategy is *Competing for the Future*, by Gary Hamel and C. K. Prahalad.
- **Voice-of-customer interviewing:** You'll need plenty of practice, but a good starting point is the four-hour virtual public workshop we developed at The AIM Institute, Everyday VOC.
- **Exploring future trends:** Kevin Kelly provides a good perspective for studying future trends in, *The Inevitable: Understanding the 12 Technological Forces That Will Shape Our Future*.
- **Jobs to be done:** This framework for understanding customer needs is thoroughly explained by Scott Burleson in *The Statue in the Stone: Decoding Customer Motivation with the 48 Laws of Jobs-to-be-Done Philosophy*.
- **Project management:** Does a Gantt chart fill you with dread or purpose? Find many resources to master this skill at the Project Management Institute.
- **Public speaking:** Builders need to inspire others, and they often do this while speaking to groups. Find a Toastmasters International Club near you, where you can hone these skills.

Where do you start? Consider what your business needs and which skills you need to improve. For me, it was public speaking. When I was in my twenties, I stood up to make a presentation and was so nervous I had to sit back down before I blacked out. After a few years in the local Toastmasters Club, I would get excited whenever someone handed me a microphone.

STARTING POINT FOR MIDDLE MANAGERS

If this is your starting point, you *could* be in a difficult position. Consider the possibilities:

1. Your senior leaders are Decorators with no reasonable prospect for this to change.
2. Your senior leaders aren't committed Builders today, but this could change.
3. Your senior leaders are Builders today.

For scenario one above, consider building the skill of resume writing. Our research shows that one-third to one-half of businesses today are led by Builders. These companies *do* exist, so why not find and join one?

Scenario two is trickier. Many years ago, a company I worked for was acquired, and I had doubts about the new management's vision for the future. At the time I was working for a Builder extraordinaire who gave me great freedom to build capabilities.

I met with the new president to compare his vision of the future with mine. Sure enough, they were very different, so

I MENTIONED THAT I WOULDN'T MIND BEING LAID OFF.

I mentioned that I wouldn't mind being laid off. This worked because (a) Decorators don't mind letting people go, and (b) severance packages were quite generous back then.

Your approach might be more nuanced. You could share the principles in this book—or the book itself—with your boss to get her reaction. Find out if there's an appetite among senior leaders for someone like you to embark on some serious business building. If the answer is good luck with that, polish up your resume.

But you may find there is interest, and *you* may be a catalyst for change. In this case, you can take many of the same steps you would working for a Builder

When you work for a Builder—scenario three—it's important to have regular touch-base meetings with them. Most

MOST BUILDERS ARE GREAT MENTORS AS WELL.

Builders are great mentors as well. That's because they like to build capabilities—not just drive results—and the most important capabilities require people-development. Good questions for you to ask include:

- What personal skills do I need to develop?
- How much latitude is there to invest in the future at the expense of near-term results?
- What business capabilities do we need to develop, and how can I help?
- What market-facing innovation projects can I work on that will excite both of us?

Depending on your job level, you may be leading new product development teams, or these teams may be reporting to you. One of the most powerful building skills you can develop is throwing all your support behind such teams.

Market-facing innovation—understanding customers' highest-priority needs and introducing a new product to satisfy them—is a fragile endeavor. It's difficult and teams are easily thrown off course. Develop your reputation as a Builder where market-facing innovation *thrives*. You can do this by

- ensuring team members get the training they need to develop their skills.
- sheltering them from growth friction (cost-cutting delays) as best you can.
- providing completely frank—but kind—feedback to improve team performance.
- giving extra attention to those well-positioned to become Builders themselves.
- publicly recognizing teams that do a good job understanding and meeting customers' needs.

INNOVATION IS FRAGILE AND MUST BE SHELTERED. BE A LEADER WHERE INNOVATION *THRIVES*.

BUSINESS BUILDERS

STARTING POINT FOR SENIOR LEADERS

In our survey, nearly all senior leaders said one of the following three described their primary passion:

- driving organic growth by delivering differentiated value to customers (Builder)
- improving operational efficiency through productivity, quality, and costs (Remodeler)
- presenting favorable financial performance and outlook to investors (Decorator)

If you're among the 32 percent self-identifying as a Remodeler, you probably have a sincere desire to make things better. It may not be a reach for you to redirect your energies to Building. In other words, you won't ignore operational efficiency going forward, but you'll now set a *new* main course: driving organic growth by delivering differentiated value to customers.

If you identify as a Decorator, the transition to Building may be more difficult. You'll need to adopt a different (much longer) time horizon and become more interested in pleasing a broader range of stakeholders—especially customers and employees—not just shareholders. But you *can* do this. You are a senior leader, after all.

What if you identified as a Builder and want to get even better at Building? In terms of improving your *business*, remember the three recommendations from chapter 12:

1. Put Builders in charge.
2. Create a Growth Capabilities Road Map.
3. Attract new investors.

The first point—put Builders in charge—needs to be amplified. It's much more important than most realize to ensure Builders are in place at all levels. This gives you a strong candidate pool to select from when promoting from within. But more important is this: poor leadership can do enormous damage by curbing long-term business performance and *especially* by driving out future Builders.

Beyond these changes for the organization, what should you *personally* do differently? In the last section for middle managers, you saw several ways to support and invigorate new product development teams. As you spend less time in backward-looking financial reviews, spend *much* more time working with new product teams. I can't think of anything you can do to send a stronger message throughout your business: *Listen up, everyone. We are in the Building business!*

SOME DISCOURAGEMENT

If you're a senior leader, I hope this book will discourage you. Specifically, I hope it will discourage you from

- making shareholder wealth your primary goal, when other stakeholders—especially customers and employees—need your best efforts.
- squandering too much time on the spectator sport of financial reviews, when you could focus on new products that will create better future reviews.
- engaging in first-domino fixation by over-using spending freezes, hiring delays, travel bans, and especially layoffs that disrupt employees' families.
- spending too much time and attention on near-term results, when you could be building long-term capabilities.
- allowing your business to descend the commodity spiral toward commoditization and irrelevance.
- treating all initiatives equally, when only market-facing innovation can provide profitable growth that is sustainable.

- developing new products and services without understanding the needs of customers in your target market segments.
- forgetting that your number one duty is to leave your business stronger than you found it.

BOOST YOUR GROWTH BY *STOPPING* THESE UNFORCED ERRORS

- Shareholder wealth as your top goal
- Too much time in financial reviews
- Spending freezes, travel bans, layoffs . . .
- Near-term results over capability-building
- Descending the Commodity Death Spiral
- Undervaluing market-facing innovation
- Failing to understand market needs
- Forgetting your first duty: *Leave your business stronger than you found it*

Strange as it may seem, your company could boost its growth simply by *stopping* some of these unforced errors that are so common today. You've seen the data now; compared to faster-growth companies, slower-growth companies tend to

- make maximizing shareholder wealth their primary goal.
- employ near-term cost controls more often.
- focus more on the current year than the longer-term.
- focus on near-term results at the expense of long-term growth capabilities.
- put Decorators in charge instead of Builders.

> **YOUR COMPANY COULD BOOST ITS GROWTH SIMPLY BY STOPPING UNFORCED ERRORS THAT ARE COMMON TODAY.**

Are you keen to boost your company's growth? Are you influenced more by new data than old habits? I invite you to exercise your position of leadership to *stop* behaviors that others consider normal today.

SOME ENCOURAGEMENT

Thankfully, we can close on a more inspiring note than, "stop doing that." I've had the privilege of working with many Builders, and I can tell you this: they enjoy their jobs *way* more than the rest.

I certainly don't expect everyone to embrace the Builder philosophy. Some will pursue personal prestige and financial reward for their own sake. That's their call.

But I hope you'll realize that Bill the Builder has a very different experience than Cal the Climber. The Builder goes to work with confidence, knowing they make a difference. They've earned the respect and even admiration of those around them. They're trusted by stakeholders to build a stronger business. They're especially trusted by employees, who have seen layoff carnage created by Decorators at other companies.

If you're early in your career, I hope you'll be inspired to become a Builder. If you have no intention of becoming a business leader, I hope you'll make your way into an organization where you can contribute to the building trade.

Perhaps you're midcareer and you've been naturally practicing the principles of Building. I hope this book encourages you to press on and helps you explain to others where you're going and why.

Are you in the C-level suite or board of directors? Do you want your company to continue its current path, or is it time to change its trajectory? Only *you* can be the force in Newton's first law of motion: "An object in motion maintains the same speed and direction unless acted upon by an outside force."

Have a serious discussion about your company's speed and direction. Imagine your company's founders are in the room with you. Wouldn't they love to see a succession of Builders continually making the company stronger than they found it?

WILL YOU JOIN ME?

You can probably tell I'm on a mission to inspire a shift away from leaders who are servants of Wall Street, willing to sacrifice their employees' well-being and their company's long-term health. We can do much better. We can put Builders in charge.

If you feel the same, you can help by

- asking your friends, students, colleagues, or subordinates to read this—or slipping a copy into your boss's office.
- leaving a review on the Amazon sales page for this book, www.ReviewBusinessBuilders.com, which will expose it to more people searching there.

Thank you!

Dan Adams

APPENDIX A
THE SPECIAL ADVANTAGES OF B2B

> "Talent is hitting the target nobody else can hit, while genius is hitting the target nobody else can see."
>
> —ARTHUR SCHOPENHAUER

APPENDIX A: **THE SPECIAL ADVANTAGES OF B2B**

Until this point, our Builder recommendations have applied to leaders of any kind of business. But if yours is a B2B company, there's good news: you have special advantages over consumer goods producers when it comes to driving profitable, sustainable growth.

To be clear, when we say business-to-business, this includes any customer that is "in business." Your customer could be another large company, but it could also be a farmer, roofer, or physician if the job to be done pertains to their livelihood.

You may remember our earlier recommendation to *understand and meet customer needs better than others*. In this appendix, you'll see why B2B companies have special advantages when it comes to the *understanding* part. And in the next appendix, you'll see highly practical ways to put these advantages to work.

FIVE B2B ADVANTAGES

Imagine your company makes hoses, both garden hoses for homeowners (B2C) and hydraulic hoses for earthmoving equipment (B2B). You plan to conduct customer interviews to better understand market needs before developing a new product.

Would an interview with a homeowner about garden hose be different than one with a Caterpillar engineer about the hydraulic hose her company uses? There are five major differences, each providing you with a potential advantage. Compared to the homeowner, your B2B customer has more

1. **Knowledge:** This comes from years of education, on-the-job training, and considerable time thinking about this job to be done at work. Your advantage? The B2B engineer is *able* to explain her needs in hydraulic hoses, providing you with

dozens of desired customer outcomes. Your garden hose conversation will be shorter and shallower.

2. **Interest:** This is high given the potential economic impact. The engineer could become a hero at work if your new product lets Caterpillar produce superior earthmoving equipment. Here's a clue on homeowner interest: you typically must *pay* them to join your focus group. Your B2B advantage is that customers are *willing* to help you design better products.

3. **Objectivity:** B2B customers are pushed into rational decision-making because they make group decisions, must follow company procedures, and are held accountable for their decisions. As evidenced by those rows and rows of rental storage units, consumers buy much they don't need. Your B2B advantage is that your customers make rational, stable decisions, *and* you understand why they made them.

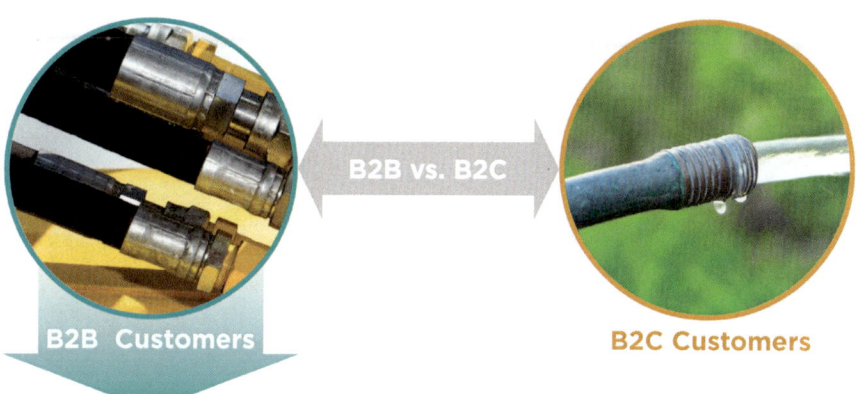

B2B Customers

- Are *able* to help you design better products (**Knowledge**)
- Are *willing* to help you design better products (**Interest**)
- Make rational, stable, understandable decisions (**Objectivity**)
- Can discuss their needs without a prototype (**Foresight**)
- Can be *engaged* and primed to buy later (**Concentration**)

BUSINESS BUILDERS

APPENDIX A: THE SPECIAL ADVANTAGES OF B2B

4. **Foresight:** B2B customers can tell you their desired *outcomes* (e.g., faster line speed, fewer defects, or extending the life of their product). They can't tell you the *solutions* needed, but this is your job, not theirs. This means you don't need to show them a product prototype before having an intelligent conversation about their needs.

5. **Concentration:** In a highly concentrated market, a B2B company has few customers, each with significant buying potential. This may not be your situation; but if it is, be sure to *impress* customers with engaging interviews and follow-through. Then they'll be primed to buy when you're ready to sell your new product.

These five are the most significant advantages, but we count a total of twelve differences between B2B and B2C. Most of these result in advantages for the B2B supplier. For a closer study, download our white paper on the subject at www.B2BvsB2C.com.

DOWNLOAD OUR WHITE PAPER WITH 12 DIFFERENCES BETWEEN B2B AND B2C AT WWW.B2BVSB2C.COM

Consider 12 differences between B2B and B2C. Many offer profound B2B growth advantages for companies that understand their implications.

THE B2B INDEX

Our hose example highlighted stark differences between B2B and B2C. But there are other cases when these labels seem inadequate. They're imprecise and sometimes misleading.

"CUSTOMERS CAN'T TELL YOU WHAT THEY WANT."

If you hear someone say this, ask if they're referring to B2B or B2C customers. If it's B2C, they may be right. Ask me what I want in a consumer video game, snack food, or men's suit... and I may need to first play with it, taste it, or try it on.

B2B customers may not be able to propose solutions, but that's not their job. It's yours. They can always tell you about their desired *outcomes*. You might hear these and dozens more when interviewing a Caterpillar engineer about hydraulic hose.

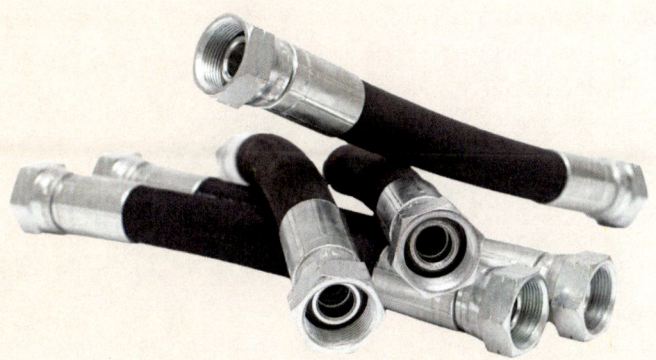

- Better cold-temp flexibility
- Higher pressure rating
- Greater diesel fuel resistance
- Tighter radius bends
- Lower weight per foot
- More hose diameters
- Reduced packaging
- Training in installation
- Faster change-out time
- Better abrasion resistance
- Fluid grit resistance
- Shorter installation time
- Reduced fading in sunlight
- Lower-weight couplings
- No leakage at couplings
- Higher temperature rating

APPENDIX A: THE SPECIAL ADVANTAGES OF B2B

Imagine your office mates send you to the store to buy a new stapler. A B2B purchase, right? But if you're like me, your knowledge, interest, and objectivity concerning staplers is rather low. I might heft a stapler to see if it feels solid, pick a color I like, and head to the cash register.

What if you've been thinking of buying a certain sports car for some time. Is your knowledge high? Your interest? And yet this is a B2C purchase. Confusing, right?

To clear things up, The AIM Institute developed the B2B index. You answer a series of online questions (at www.B2Bmarketview.com) pertaining to the five major B2B versus B2C differences: knowledge, interest, objectivity, foresight, and concentration.

The market segment you describe is then assigned a B2B index from one to one hundred. The higher the B2B index, the "more B2B" your market is. In fact, this is a measure of

THE HIGHER THE B2B INDEX, THE "MORE B2B" YOUR MARKET IS.

customer *engagement potential*. In markets with a high B2B index, like our hydraulic hose example, you can fully engage customers to understand their needs.

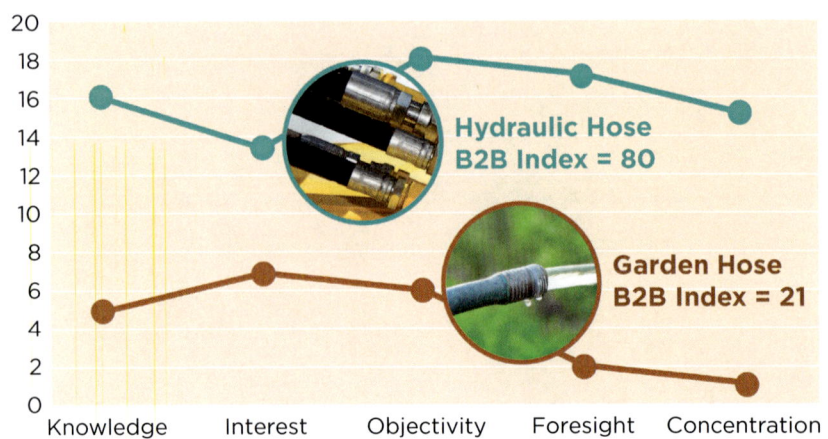

164

This illustration shows how the B2B index is calculated for two markets: hydraulic hose for earthmoving equipment and garden hose for home use. If you're responsible for multiple markets, you should run the analysis on each market segment—they may have very different B2B indices.

If you have a B2B index of forty to fifty or higher, you'll find the tips in Appendix B helpful for understanding customer needs. Even if you're selling to end-consumers (B2C), you may have a sufficiently high B2B index for these B2B suggestions. Perhaps you sell tools for working on car engines. Even though a shade tree mechanic is technically a B2C customer, his knowledge, interest, objectivity, and foresight will likely be quite high.

THE INSIGHT GAP

But wait, there's more. You have an even greater advantage if you are a B2B producer, which can be explained by *insight gaps*. Let's contrast the market insights of a tissue producer selling to consumers (B2C) with a pigment producer selling to paper producers (B2B). In the following illustration, we plot each producer's ability to understand customer needs all the way from "guessing" to "certainty."

The B2C tissue producer has reasonably high *typical insight*. Tissue designers are consumers themselves, so they have some understanding of customer needs. Also, B2C market research budgets tend to be high, which boosts typical insight. But the tissue producer has limited *potential insight*, due to low customer knowledge, interest, objectivity, foresight, and concentration (KIOFC).

Contrast this with a B2B pigment producer with low *typical insight*. This producer knows little about any of its many pigment markets (e.g., paper, paint, plastic, and pharmaceuticals). B2B

APPENDIX A: THE SPECIAL ADVANTAGES OF B2B

producers are notoriously frugal in paying for market research, which also contributes to a low typical insight. The B2B pigment producer's *potential insight*, though, is very high given the knowledge, interest, and so on of paper producers.

The insight gap is the difference between *typical* market insight and *potential* market insight. As you see, this gap is much greater for the B2B company. This large insight gap should scream one thing for most B2B companies—*Opportunity*! You and your competitors know far less about customer needs than you *could* know. If you close this gap before competitors, you'll turbocharge your profitable, sustainable growth.

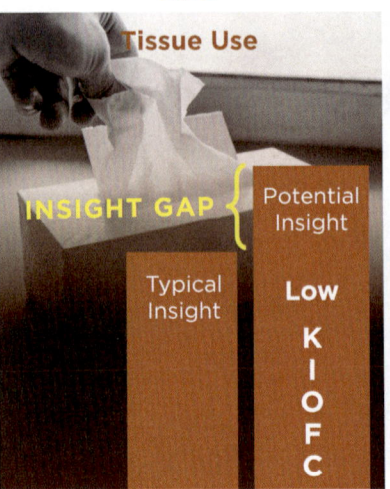
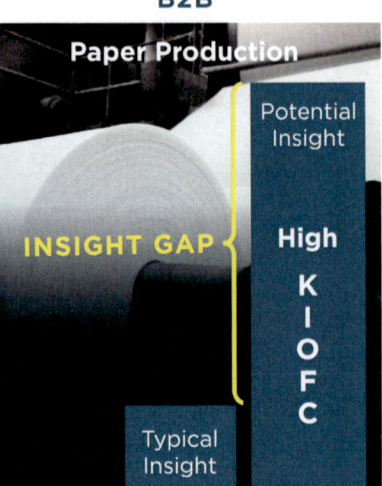

THE "FASTER HORSE" FALLACY

When Steve Jobs was asked why Apple didn't conduct more customer interviews, he quoted Henry Ford: "If I had asked my customers what they wanted, they would have told me a faster horse." Or maybe you've heard this: "Customers can't tell you what they want."

But this is flawed thinking for two reasons. First, as you've now seen, B2B companies have much greater potential to understand customer needs. Second, the phrase "what customers want" overlooks the important distinction between outcomes and solutions.

"IF I HAD ASKED MY CUSTOMERS WHAT THEY WANTED, THEY WOULD HAVE TOLD ME A FASTER HORSE."

—Henry Ford

Your B2B interviews should only focus on customer *outcomes*, that is, their desired end-results. Don't talk about solutions in the front end of innovation because this may jeopardize your ownership of intellectual property later. And it wastes precious time you could spend exploring the customers' job to be done and its corresponding outcomes.

Customers understand their outcomes. Suppliers understand their solutions. You need to enter the customer's world to learn about their outcomes. Don't ask customers to enter your world to help with solutions.

DON'T ASK CUSTOMERS TO ENTER YOUR WORLD TO HELP WITH SOLUTIONS.

Imagine you worked for Apple when it created the first iPod. If you had interviewed customers, you might have heard them say they wanted to

- take their music wherever they travel.
- share their music with others.

- be able to organize their music.
- purchase one song at a time.
- listen to music while exercising.
- find similar songs to the current one.

These are *outcomes*. They are *what* customers want, not *how* customers will become satisfied. If you knew which outcomes were most important and unsatisfied, you'd know exactly what to target in your solution. The solutions keep coming: record players, transistor radios, Sony Walkman, CDs, iPods, music streaming, and so on.

And that faster horse and Ford Model T? Those were just solutions too. If you develop your solutions without knowing which outcomes customers care about, you might get lucky every now and then. But you can certainly do better, as we'll describe in the next appendix.

APPLY A B2B VERSUS B2C FILTER

When it comes to innovation practices, thought leaders will continue bringing you new ideas to consider, many of which will be worth a serious look. But one caution: use a B2B versus B2C filter when considering new approaches to market-facing innovation.

When faced with a new methodology, your first question should be, *How will this work given my five B2B advantages?* You'll probably find some elements of the new methodology that are valuable. But you may also find useless or even damaging portions you need to eliminate or revise.

As an example, take Lean Startup, an innovation framework popularized by Eric Reis in his book *The Lean Startup: How*

USE A B2B VERSUS B2C FILTER WHEN CONSIDERING NEW APPROACHES TO INNOVATION.

Today's Entrepreneurs Use Continuous Innovation to Create Radically Successful Businesses.[43] There's much to like about it:

- You avoid elaborate business plans, which limit openness to learning.
- You create a business model canvas, a visual template to organize assumptions and learn which to test.
- You employ "pivot or persevere" points in combination with agile, a project management methodology characterized by short work sprints and frequent adaptation.
- You generate minimum viable products for rapid customer feedback.

But for B2B innovation, should we use Lean Startup as-is, straight out of the box? Probably not. Lean Startup uses the build-measure-learn cycle, which makes sense if your B2C customers don't know what they want until you "build" a prototype (minimum viable product) and show it to them.

But if your B2B customers have high knowledge, interest, objectivity, and foresight, why would you ever start building something without first having an intelligent conversation to understand their needs? Keep this cycle, but *start* with a learn

BUSINESS BUILDERS

OUTCOMES VERSUS SOLUTIONS

It's critical to understand the difference between customer outcomes and supplier solutions. An outcome is the customers' desired end result.

A solution is just one way to deliver desired outcomes. Don't spend any time on these during your front-end customer interviews.

Customers "own" outcome space and suppliers "own" solution space. Once you understand customer outcomes, you can develop solutions.

Outcomes are often stable over time. But solutions come and go, in this case from record players to music streaming. What will the next innovation be? All we know is it will address outcome(s) that are important and not yet satisfied.

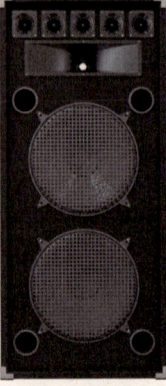

CUSTOMERS KNOW OUTCOMES

- Make music portable
- Share my music
- Organize my music
- Purchase singles
- Listen while exercising
- Find similar songs

SUPPLIERS PROVIDE SOLUTIONS

- Record players
- Transistor radios
- Sony Walkman
- CDs
- iPods
- Music streaming

LEAN STARTUP'S BUILD-MEASURE-LEARN CYCLE

step. This "learning" is accomplished with the qualitative and quantitative B2B-optimized interviews covered in Appendix B.

When B2B companies blindly follow Lean Startup without applying a B2B versus B2C filter, they can miss three additional points:

1. Customers will be more engaged and eager to work with you if you first ask *their* opinion instead of touting *your* idea.
2. Some consumer product prototypes—a new soft drink flavor or software demo—could be faster and cheaper to build than some complex B2B prototypes.
3. B2C companies have a deeper pool of testers than B2B. Don't frustrate a small set of important B2B customers by lobbing careless prototypes at them.

My point isn't to avoid Lean Startup or anything else that comes along. Just evaluate it carefully, so you don't discard your B2B advantages.

AN ADVANTAGE IS NO ADVANTAGE UNLESS YOU TAKE ADVANTAGE OF IT.

BUSINESS BUILDERS

APPENDIX A: **THE SPECIAL ADVANTAGES OF B2B**

You now understand the most important advantages for a B2B company. But an advantage is no advantage unless you take advantage of it. In Appendix B, we'll use these advantages to give your market-facing innovation a powerful boost.

APPENDIX B
HOW TO UNDERSTAND B2B CUSTOMER NEEDS

> "Cheating on customer discovery interviews is like cheating in your parachute packing class."
>
> —STEVE BLANK

APPENDIX B: **HOW TO UNDERSTAND B2B CUSTOMER NEEDS**

You should be rewarded for your diligence in reaching this final chapter. And you will be, because I've saved some incredibly potent how-to suggestions until the end.

For this chapter, I'll assume you want to be a highly successful, admired, and trusted Builder in a B2B company. You want to drive profitable, sustainable growth from market-facing innovation.

I'll further assume that you understand you need to build the right capabilities and that this is a multi-year endeavor. But still. You'd *really* like a fast-moving, tangible plan of attack that will

- create the shortest and most efficient path to significantly better growth.
- be based on hard evidence—not guesswork—that superior growth will result.
- inspire key stakeholders, especially employees, customers, and shareholders.

I was conflicted about including this appendix, because it covers training that my company, The AIM Institute, has offered B2B companies since 2005—something called New Product Blueprinting. On one hand, I didn't want to "taint" our message on leadership with crass commercialism. If that's a danger, please stop reading now and begin applying the Builder lessons you've learned.

I KNOW OF NOTHING ELSE THAT COMES EVEN CLOSE TO DELIVERING SUCH IMPRESSIVE B2B GROWTH.

On the other hand, I know of nothing else that comes even close to delivering such impressive B2B growth as what I'll describe next. It's a B2B-optimized approach to understand customer needs better than others. Today, relatively few B2B companies use it, so you could gain a strong competitive advantage.

This approach involves three steps:

1. **Discovery interviews:** You begin with a round of qualitative, divergent interviews to uncover all customer outcomes in your target market segment. This eliminates *errors of omission*—failing to uncover unarticulated needs.
2. **Preference interview:** Next you conduct a round of quantitative, convergent interviews to get one to ten importance and satisfaction ratings on key customer outcomes. You need this to eliminate *errors of commission*—choosing the wrong outcomes to improve.
3. **Market Satisfaction Gaps:** The MSG chart lets your team focus on the highest gaps—outcomes that are important to the customer and not being satisfied. This lets you avoid *errors of bias*—allowing wishful thinking, pre-conceptions, and internal filtering to degrade your product design.

Before exploring each step, let's take a high-level view of actions that reduce commercial risk in B2B market-facing innovation.

HOW TO LOWER COMMERCIAL RISK

In chapter 10, you saw how commercial risk has been the leading cause of new product failure for five decades. You learned that B2B companies can build a Certainty Time Machine to approach commercial certainty in the front end of innovation. This lets them deal primarily with technical risk in the costly development stage.

What would this mean for your company? Imagine if your engineers, chemists, or software developers were handed a precise set of customer outcomes to pursue for each new product. They'd *know* their new product would be successful if they could just satisfy these outcomes. Wouldn't you see improvements *everywhere*—your new product success rate, your vitality index,[44] your profit margins, and your organic growth rate?

APPENDIX B: **HOW TO UNDERSTAND B2B CUSTOMER NEEDS**

What does reducing commercial risk look like? For the highest level of commercial risk, you *guess* what customers want. Don't laugh; this "voice of ourselves" approach is popular in many B2B companies today.

In the following illustration, actions two through eleven progressively reduce commercial risk from this "guessing" level. In actions three through six, you broaden the range of job functions and companies to interview within your target market segment. Without this, you might design a new product for an "outlier" person or company instead of the entire market segment.

Actions seven through nine cover elements of qualitative Discovery interviews, action ten covers B2B customer observation, and action eleven addresses quantitative Preference interviews. Spoiler alert: the single most impactful action you can take is the one you're probably skipping today: action eleven—Preference interviews.

HOW TO **LOWER** B2B COMMERCIAL RISK

1.	*Guess* what customers want.
2.	Ask your sales reps what customers want.
3.	Ask one job function at one customer account.
4.	Interview many job functions and customers.
5.	Interview your customers' customers.
6.	Interview the entire market ecosystem.
7.	Let customers lead Discovery interviews.
8.	Use advanced interview probing questions.
9.	Generate fresh ideas with trigger methods.
10.	Observe customers' processes during tours.
11.	Conduct quantitative Preference interviews.

Perhaps you've seen "Choose Your Own Adventure" books. In market-facing innovation, you get to choose your own level of commercial risk. To virtually eliminate it in the front end of B2B innovation, follow these three steps: Discovery interviews, Preference interviews, and Market Satisfaction Gaps.

DISCOVERY INTERVIEWS

B2C interviewers have a single objective: customer insight. But if yours is a concentrated B2B market—with a few customers that could each purchase a lot—you have a second objective: customer *engagement*.

In other words, you want to conduct your voice-of-customer interviews in a highly respectful, peer-to-peer manner. (No watching customers through a one-way mirror as they answer questions.) After an interview, customers should say, "Wow, a supplier that *listened* to us. That's the kind of company we'd like to work with."

What does a good B2B Discovery interview look like? Here's a five-minute video that provides an example of an ingredient supplier interviewing a paint customer: www.VOCforB2B.com. You'll notice many of these characteristics:

1. **Use a top team.** Don't send "hired guns" to interview. Take your own team—with a technical representative—so customers know they're talking to someone who can innovate for them.
2. **Drop the questionnaire.** Never bore customers with a questionnaire or survey. How excited are you when someone comes to your front door asking you to complete a survey?
3. **Project your notes.** Display customers' comments on a screen or during a web-conference, so they can see them, make corrections, and "own" the conversation.

APPENDIX B: **HOW TO UNDERSTAND B2B CUSTOMER NEEDS**

DISCOVERY INTERVIEWS

Imagine you make corrugated boxes, and you are interviewing Amazon about their packaging needs. Display your notes so you can engage them, and they can correct you. Record one customer outcome per sticky note and probe well with

- **"What"** questions: *Can you describe that? When does this happen? How often does this happen? Where does it occur?*

- **"Why"** questions: *Why is this a problem? Can you describe the impact?*

After each outcome ask: *Any other problems?* You'll have no idea what outcome the next sticky note will hold. Your customer leads the interview—not you—so you'll learn much more than with a questionnaire.

This B2B-optimized approach engages customers and teaches you what you didn't know you didn't know.

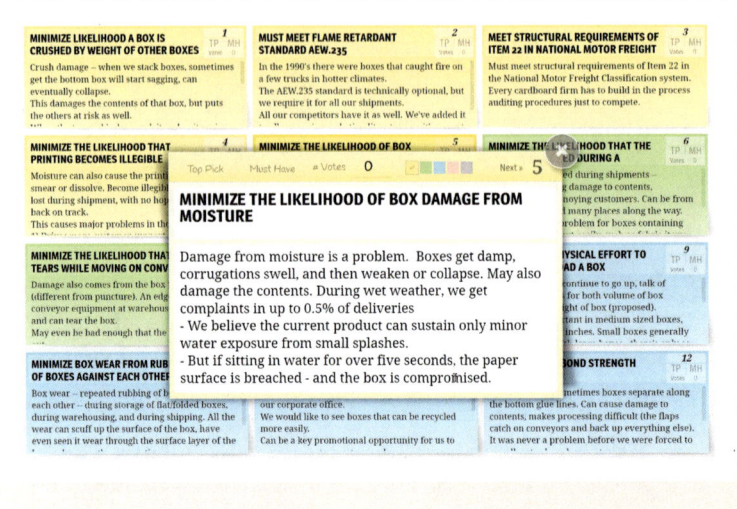

4. **Assign roles.** Your moderator asks most of the questions and your notetaker records customer comments. An optional observer can help the moderator by also asking good probing questions.

5. **Focus on the customer.** Discuss only the customer's desired outcomes, not your products. In these interviews, it's all about customers and their needs.

6. **Don't discuss hypotheses.** Don't "lead the witness" to validate your concepts. Customers may sense you are more interested in *confirming* your ideas than in *understanding* their needs.

7. **Multiple job functions.** Consider which customer job functions influence or make buying decisions for your type of product. Try to interview them at the same time.

8. **Don't sell or solve.** If you try to sell, customers will think your "interview" was just a sales gimmick. If you start solving, you could jeopardize your intellectual property later.

9. **Trigger more ideas.** Spark fresh thinking with *trigger maps*. For example, a map could display trends that might impact the customer's future. This helps generate more outcomes.

10. **Probe skillfully.** Signal your interest and learn more by recapping, making affirming comments, and probing with "what" and "why" questions.

11. **Let customers lead.** After customers give you a desired outcome (and you understand it), simply ask "What else?" This lets your customer discuss outcomes *they* care about.

Conducting Discovery interviews in this manner puts you in a position to be *surprised*. Granted, most businesspeople don't want to be surprised. Would *you* while installing new software, traveling on business, or building a new facility?

YOU WANT TO BE SURPRISED BY CUSTOMER NEEDS YOUR COMPETITORS HAVE MISSED.

APPENDIX B: HOW TO UNDERSTAND B2B CUSTOMER NEEDS

But innovation is the exception. You can't even get a patent unless your idea is new, useful, and *nonobvious*, that is, surprising. Don't just look for surprises in the lab. Allow yourself to be surprised by customer needs that competitors have missed.

I was having a tough time convincing one team to ditch their customer questionnaire. Finally, I said:

- You know what you know. (facts)
- You know what you think. (hypotheses)
- And you know what you don't know. (questions)
- But you *don't know what you don't know*.

The spark of innovation often comes from these surprises, which are unlikely to surface from fill-in-the-blank questionnaires and interview guides. With Discovery interviews, customers lead you to what's important to them—and often surprising to you.

We surveyed 397 clients we had trained in this interview methodology and who had then completed more than 1,800 Discovery interviews in total. (You can download this research at www.BlueprintingDiscovery.com.) Ninety percent reported

SURVEY RESPONSES TO "WE LEARNED UNEXPECTED INFORMATION DURING DISCOVERY INTERVIEWS."

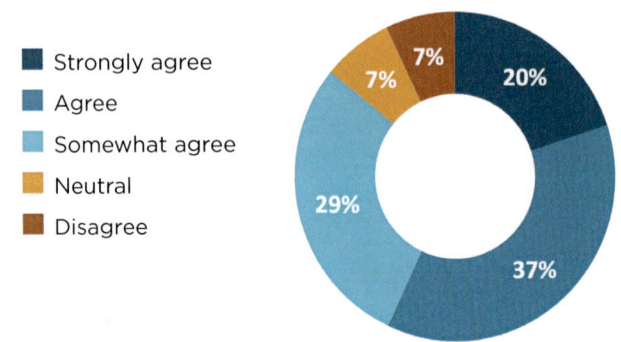

- Strongly agree
- Agree
- Somewhat agree
- Neutral
- Disagree

the interviews helped them gain a deeper understanding of customer needs, and 88 percent said they learned more valuable information than in typical customer interactions. But the best part was that many learned *unexpected* information (see chart).

PREFERENCE INTERVIEWS

A frustrated marketing professional once approached me with this story. He had completed five months of voice-of-customer interviews and presented his findings to his boss, who said, "No, I don't think customers want *that*. I think they want *this*." I asked if he had conducted quantitative VOC interviews, or just qualitative. He replied, "Just qualitative."

> **THAT LAME OUTCOME SHOWS UP IN MY PRESENTATION AS A CUSTOMER QUOTE IN SEVENTY-TWO-POINT BOLD ARIAL FONT.**

Qualitative-only VOC isn't convincing because we often hear what we want to hear. Perhaps the outcome I *hoped* to hear was offered by just one customer as an afterthought. But that lame outcome shows up in my presentation as a customer quote in seventy-two-point bold Arial font. Hey, the customer *did* say they wanted this, right?

Preference interviews avoid this problem by communicating needs directly from the customer to supplier in a quantified, unfiltered, unbiased fashion. Imagine you're a packaging supplier, and your recently completed Discovery interviews uncovered outcomes such as:

- Minimize the likelihood of box damage from moisture.
- Maximize the percent of recyclable content in new boxes.
- Minimize the frequency of crushed boxes due to vertical loading.

During Preference interviews, you then ask two questions for each outcome: (a) how important is this outcome? and (b) how satisfied are you today with your ability to achieve it? Here are some best practices for Preference interviews.

1. **Anchor responses.** Interpret the one to ten importance and satisfaction rating numbers for customers. On the importance scale, equate five and ten to "moderately important" and "critical," respectively. For the satisfaction scale, anchor five and ten as "barely acceptable" and "totally satisfied," respectively.

2. **Engage all functions.** Conduct interviews with all customer job functions together (e.g., manufacturing, technical, marketing) that would normally influence the buying decision. If they disagree on a one to ten rating, let them debate so you can learn more. If they still can't agree ask: "How important is this outcome from the perspective of your *entire company*?"

3. **Display your notes.** As shown in the sidebar, it helps to digitally project your notes to engage customers. Just as you did in Discovery interviews, probe for better understanding. Display these notes so customers can correct you as needed.

4. **Never force-rank.** Don't ask customers to rank outcomes from most important to least important. That reveals the *relative* desirability of each outcome, and you want their *absolute* desirability. If the market is overserved—not eager for *any* improvements—force-ranking will still lead you to work on *something*. It implicitly encourages all projects to continue even when some should be killed.

Preference interviews are key to *prioritizing* customer needs, telling you which outcomes to work on, and which to pass on. We conducted a survey (n=311) to better understand which of twelve B2B voice-of-customer skills were most impactful. (You can download this research at www.B2BVOCSkills.com.)

PREFERENCE INTERVIEWS

After Discovery interviews, you conduct Preference interviews—usually with the same customers—on the most popular outcomes you heard during your Discovery interviews.

You ask customers to rate each outcome on a one to ten scale for importance and satisfaction. You should "anchor" your numerical scale with text descriptions so that all interviewees interpret ratings the same.

These results are then averaged for the entire market in a Market Satisfaction Gap chart, where the highest Gaps identify outcomes that are *most important* and *least satisfied*.

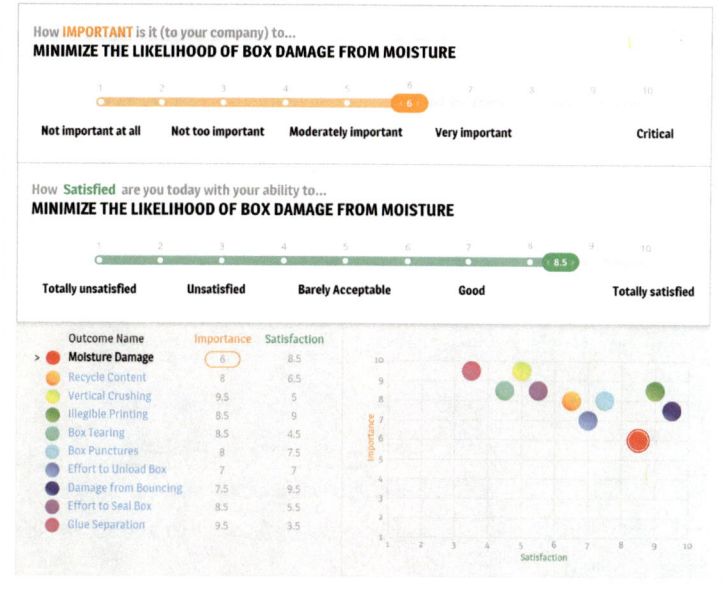

BUSINESS BUILDERS

APPENDIX B: HOW TO UNDERSTAND B2B CUSTOMER NEEDS

As shown in the following illustration, respondents not only evaluated their competency in these VOC skills, they also reported their personal success rate in new product development:

- I am rarely successful. (light bar at top)
- I am successful half the time. (medium density bar)
- I am usually successful. (dark bar at the bottom)

What was the strongest differentiator between those *rarely* and *usually* successful in new product development? It was *prioritizing customer needs*. This is accomplished with Preference interviews. Sadly, most B2B companies fail to conduct such interviews.

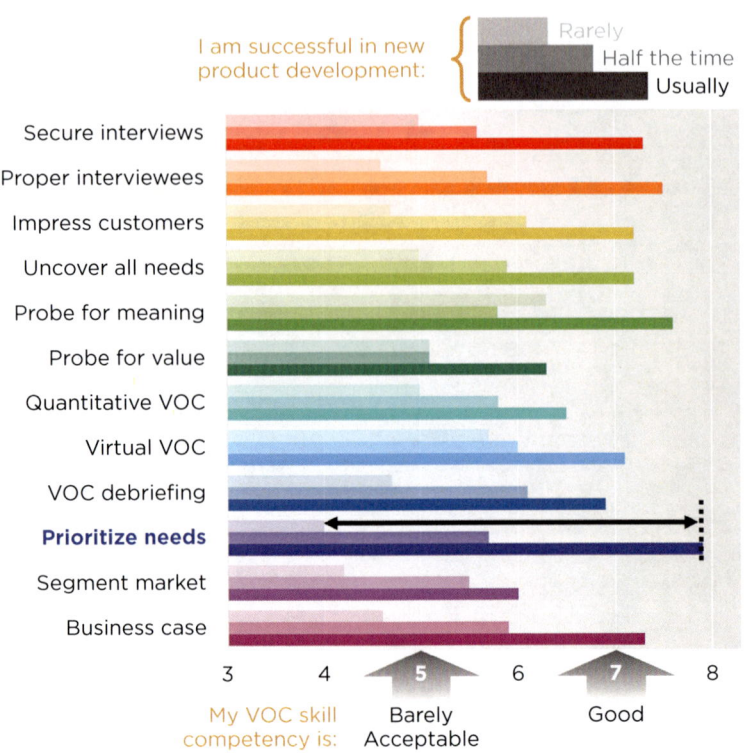

We were surprised to see that prioritizing customer needs surpassed the other eleven VOC skills in other areas as well. It was rated as:

- The most important by all respondents.
- That which unskilled respondents were most eager to improve.
- The biggest differentiator in understanding market needs.
- The skill that improved the most with VOC training.

> **WE STOPPED COUNTING THE NUMBER OF TEAMS THAT *COMPLETELY* CHANGED THEIR VIEW OF MARKET NEEDS AFTER PREFERENCE INTERVIEWS.**

This wasn't a total shock to us. Long ago we stopped counting the number of teams that *completely* changed their view of market needs after Preference interviews. Their aha moment typically comes while examining their Market Satisfaction Gap chart.

MARKET SATISFACTION GAPS

A Market Satisfaction Gap chart is created directly from your Preference interviews. Those one to ten importance (IMP) and satisfaction (SAT) ratings are averaged for all customers interviewed in your target market. If your market is highly concentrated, you should weight each company response according to its buying power.

Market Satisfaction Gaps are calculated using this simple formula:

Market Satisfaction Gap = Average Importance Rating x (10 - Average Satisfaction Rating)

If the average market importance rating is nine and the average satisfaction rating is six, your Market Satisfaction Gap for this outcome is 9 x (10 - 6) = 36 percent.

We introduced this methodology in 2005 and have used it with thousands of B2B new product teams around the world. Here's what we've learned: if an outcome scores a Gap of ~30 percent or more, it means the market is eager for improvement. These are the outcomes you should pursue. After all, the only

IF AN OUTCOME SCORES A GAP OF ~30 PERCENT OR MORE, IT MEANS THE MARKET IS EAGER FOR IMPROVEMENT.

way to get a price premium is to improve something important (high IMP rating) that needs improving (low SAT rating).

The higher the Market Satisfaction Gap, the more eager the market is for improvement. Our research shows nearly half of all projects have at least one outcome scoring 50 percent or more. These markets are begging for help. Of course, most suppliers don't know this because they don't conduct Preference interviews.

What if all outcomes score well below 30 percent? This is called an *overserved* market. Most teams stop pursuing these markets because customers just want a lower price. Instead, the team pivots to a different market segment eager for improvements.

You might think new product teams can "sense" market needs without Preference interviews and Market Satisfaction Gap charts. This sometimes happens, but not often. We studied fifty project teams that had completed a total of 875 Discovery and Preference interviews. (You can download this research at www.BlueprintingPreference.com.)

Since 90 percent of these interviews were conducted in familiar markets, you'd expect teams' initial product design ideas would be mostly *confirmed* after these interviews. But this was the case for only 16 percent of the teams. The remaining 84 percent said these interviews had a "great" or "significant" impact on their product design. If your business isn't conducting such interviews, it's likely that five out of six of *your* teams would also change their product design with Discovery- and Preference-induced customer insights.

MARKET SATISFACTION GAPS

Market Satisfaction Gaps—introduced by The AIM Institute in 2005—have helped thousands of teams confidently create product designs.

They are calculated based on the market-averaged one to ten importance (IMP) and satisfaction (SAT) ratings gathered in preference interviews:

MSG = Average IMP x (10 – Average SAT)

If the market's IMP rating is nine and SAT rating is six, the Market Satisfaction Gap for this outcome is

9 x (10 – 6) = 36 percent.

The market is eager to see improvement in outcomes with Gaps of ~30 percent or more.

BUSINESS BUILDERS

APPENDIX B: HOW TO UNDERSTAND B2B CUSTOMER NEEDS

SURVEY RESPONSES TO "HOW MUCH HAVE THESE INTERVIEWS IMPACTED THE DESIGN OF YOUR NEW OFFERING?"

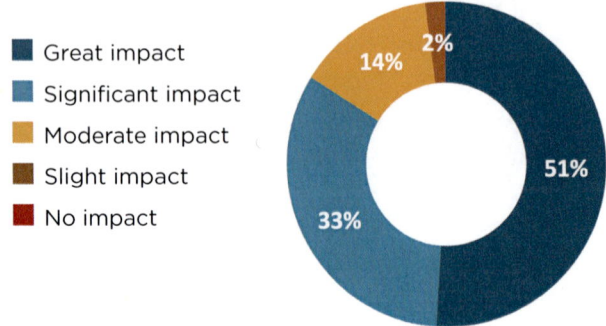

- Great impact
- Significant impact
- Moderate impact
- Slight impact
- No impact

Preference interviews and Market Satisfaction Gaps are particularly useful in overcoming confirmation bias. This is seeking and interpreting data in a manner that supports one's preconceived notions. It's more powerful than you might imagine, and it is *lethal* to innovation.

Scientists tell us that our brains get a shot of "feel-good" dopamine with every confirmation we hear. Unless you can control your brain chemistry, you'll need strong countermeasures. For starters, make sure you're not falling into any of these traps that support confirmation bias:

- starting a project with your solution(s)
- asking customers to "validate" your idea(s)
- failing to identify and test key assumptions
- skipping quantitative interviews

Would you like to add R&D staff that understands your technology, won't cost you more, and can start work tomorrow? Simple—kill your dead-end projects to free up R&D staff for truly valuable projects.

Which projects do you kill? That's hard to say today. But if you use Market Satisfaction Gaps, you'll start killing future projects in the front end *before* your R&D even sees them.

WOULD YOU LIKE TO ADD R&D STAFF THAT UNDERSTANDS YOUR TECHNOLOGY, WON'T COST YOU MORE, AND CAN START WORK TOMORROW?

OBSERVATION ON CUSTOMER TOURS

We find that B2B new product teams learn most of what they need to know through these Discovery and Preference interviews. But they can also learn a good deal through observation.

MARGARET MEAD OBSERVED, "WHAT PEOPLE SAY, WHAT PEOPLE DO, AND WHAT THEY SAY THEY DO ARE ENTIRELY DIFFERENT THINGS."

Margaret Mead observed, "What people say, what people do, and what they say they do are entirely different things." For this reason, many market researchers like to practice *ethnography*: the study of people's behaviors and customs. For some consumer goods markets with a low B2B index (little engagement potential), it can even be the *primary* mode of insight.

Observation has a place in B2B markets, often taking the form of a supplier touring their customer's facility. Some good practices here include:

- Allow an hour for the tour.
- If possible, conduct the tour before your Discovery interview to give you good context.
- Ask your host to draw a sketch before the tour so you can orient yourself.
- Before asking questions of a worker, get permission from your host (for safety reasons).

APPENDIX B: HOW TO UNDERSTAND B2B CUSTOMER NEEDS

"DISCOVERY CONSISTS OF SEEING WHAT EVERYBODY HAS SEEN AND THINKING WHAT NOBODY HAS THOUGHT."

—Albert Szent-Gyorgyi

Your goal is to learn as much as you can. Your "fresh eyes" might spot a workaround or inefficiency your customers can no longer "see."

At The AIM Institute, we developed the AMUSE methodology to help uncover possible areas of improvement. During your tour, observe the customers' process as a series of discrete activities. Then look for ways to **A**ccelerate each activity, **M**inimize input (capital, material, labor, energy), **U**pgrade output, **S**implify transitions, or **E**liminate an activity altogether.

IMPROVING E-COMMERCE PACKAGING WITH AMUSE CUSTOMER TOUR METHOD

Accelerate Activity
Minimize Input
Upgrade Output
Simplify Transition
Eliminate Activity

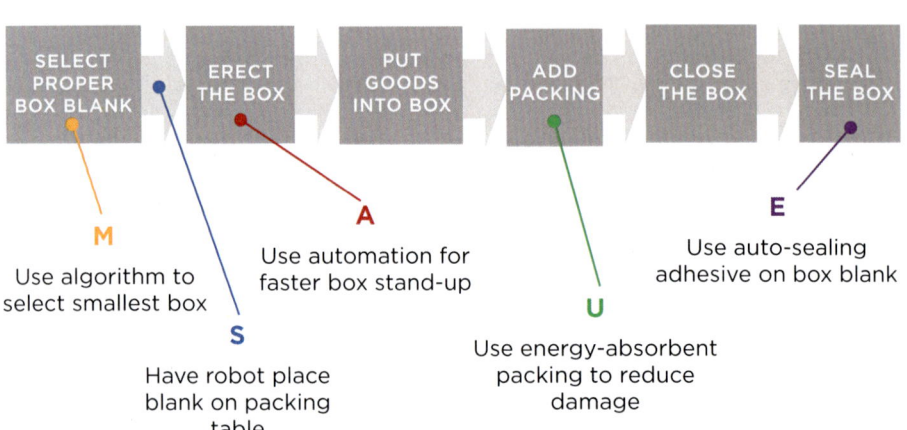

Like any new skill, this takes practice. But it's truly impressive to see what a skilled team can learn using this approach.

CLOSING THOUGHTS

I've had the privilege of working with many of the largest B2B companies around the world, and here's what I see: there is an enormous chasm between "normal practice" today and "what could be."

Don't take this as a note of discouragement. It's not. Rather it speaks to the upside potential for a B2B company led by a determined Builder. I doubt many can even imagine the level of profitable, sustainable growth that can be achieved. This is especially true for a company that "gets it" before its competitors.

> **I DOUBT MANY CAN EVEN IMAGINE THE LEVEL OF PROFITABLE, SUSTAINABLE GROWTH THAT CAN BE ACHIEVED.**

Such a company will understand and prioritize customer needs in one market segment after another. They'll launch product after product that customers love. Competitors will wonder how this company keeps hitting the bullseye while they keep missing. It almost seems unfair.

I'll leave you with two recommendations if you choose this journey. The first is to begin changing your culture. Peter Drucker said, "Culture eats strategy for breakfast." You may find my series of fifty (free) two-minute videos on B2B organic growth helpful for this, at www.B2Bgrowth.video.

The second is to announce a target date for a new game-changing innovation standard. This is when you will no longer allow any substantial new product projects to enter the costly development stage without a Market Satisfaction Gap chart (or similar). What constitutes substantial? A good starting point is any project requiring at least twelve person-months of development.

As a Builder, you know there is much to do. But these two steps will tell your organization where you're going and why you're going there. You'll lay the foundation for a building program few have ever seen. You'll know your business will become stronger than you found it. You'll be an admired and trusted Builder.

ACKNOWLEDGMENTS

If you've found this book helpful, it's only right that I pull back the curtain to reveal the many friends that made it possible, and to whom I am deeply grateful.

First, let me thank the *researchers*, without whom this would have simply been a collection of my opinions and musings. Gina O'Connor—Professor of Innovation Management at Babson College and noted author—co-created the research survey with me that's been cited throughout this book. Thank you, Gina!

Scott Burleson, my dear friend and colleague at The AIM Institute, skillfully built the survey instrument. And several friends at important associations helped gather the responses—Lee Green at Innovation Research Interchange (IRI) and Rand Mendez and Lynn Yanyo at the Institute for the Study of Business Markets (ISBM).

Second, I'm grateful for those who helped *craft* the book itself. Liz Harr and Rowena Figueroa of Hinge Marketing were my constant and insightful guides. Christian Baldo, also of Hinge Marketing, provided the design for the book cover and general layout.

My good friend Craig Palenshus was the design master behind more than one hundred book graphics and final layout. I'm indebted as well to my editor, Laura Kaiser of Word Haven Editorial, and proofreader, Melissa Stevens of Purple Ninja Editorial.

Finally, I want to thank those who *inspired* me to write this book. Since the late 1970s, I've learned so many lessons working for men and women who were Builders at heart. They include Bill Niederst, Tom Waltermire, John Carbone, John Weaver, Sarah Coffin and Kees Verhaar. We didn't know it at the time, but they were building chapters while they were building businesses.

There would be no book at all without my high school sweetheart and wife, Carol. As she has done for nearly five decades, she encouraged me every step of the way. And she did this knowing that she would also be my main muse and editor, refining each draft before others saw it.

Finally, I am grateful to the Lord for leading me to write this. In Matthew 22:37, Jesus says, "Let your light so shine before others, so that they may see your *good works and give glory to your Father* who is in heaven."

What good works could possibly come from a *business* book? I hope it contributes to a change in how employees are treated. I don't believe we should consider it "normal" for employees and their families to be discharged and uprooted in the pursuit of forgettable quarterly earnings. My highest hope for this book is that we'll see more Business Builders that feel the same.

ABOUT THE AUTHOR

As founder and president of The AIM Institute—and one of the world's foremost experts in B2B innovation—Dan Adams has trained tens of thousands of global B2B professionals. He has continually refined AIM's B2B-optimized voice-of-customer methods, as project teams in every conceivable B2B industry around the world applied them in the crucible of real-world practice.

In recent years, Dan and his team have conducted significant original research into the behaviors that drive B2B organic growth. He works with leadership teams at the largest B2B firms in the world, helping them craft dependable road maps to profitable, sustainable organic growth.

Dan is the author of *New Product Blueprinting: The Handbook for B2B Organic Growth*, the video series *B2B Organic Growth* (www.b2bgrowth.video), and the *Awkward Realities* microblog (www.awkwardrealities.com).

He has received numerous innovation awards, including a listing in the National Inventors Hall of Fame, and is a fellow at the Institute for the Study of Business Markets. An award-winning speaker, he has lectured at Wharton's Executive MBA program and other American and European universities and is a popular industry keynote speaker.

ABOUT AIM INSTITUTE

The AIM Institute (www.theaiminstitute.com) is a training firm that helps large B2B companies grow larger. We help you drive profitable, sustainable organic growth in these ways:

New Product Blueprinting: We train your marketing, product management, and technical professionals to understand B2B market needs *before* they begin the costly development stage. Backed by years of research on its effectiveness, Blueprinting is the world's leading B2B voice-of-customer method today. (www.NewProductBlueprinting.com)

Everyday VOC®: We train your B2B sales professionals—and others interacting with customers—in our advanced probing methods. This leads to more sales today and lets you capture rich insights for CRM data mining later. It's a great supplement to other sales training and for your annual sales meetings. (www.EverydayVOCtraining.com)

Minesweeper® Project De-Risking: Do you have a transformational project with a new market or technology? This lets you defuse any project-killing "landmines" early—or halt the project quickly. You'll identify, rate, and investigate assumptions in a way that boosts management confidence. (www.deriskprojects.com)

Free B2B Growth Videos: Real change takes place when your business *culture* changes. These fifty free two-minute video lessons from Dan Adams promote a Builder's mindset for growth. Employees and MBA students can sign up at www.b2bGrowth.Video to receive new lessons daily or weekly.

To tell us about *your* needs, contact us at www.talkwithaim.com.

ORDERING BOOKS

This book is available in hard cover, paperback, and Kindle versions from Amazon at www.BusinessBuildersAmazon.com.

Want larger quantities for your employees or MBA class? Paperback copies are available at a discount for quantities of ten or more. Just tell us your needs at www.talkwithaim.com.

ENDNOTES

1. This survey was conducted in May–June 2022, with responses coming from mailing list recipients of three organizations (Innovation Research Interchange, Institute for the Study of Business Markets, and the AIM Institute) and LinkedIn contacts of the book author and AIM Institute colleagues. Responses included company employees at the levels of individual contributor (n=146), middle manager (n=356), and senior leader (n=152). Some companies represented were publicly traded (n=465) while others were privately held (n=189). The companies had annual revenue of less than $50 million (n=116), $50–$500 million (n=222), $0.5–$2 billion (n=136), $2–$5 billion (n=69), and over $5 billion (n=111). These companies were headquartered in North America (n=409), Europe (n=145), Asia (n=50), and the rest-of-the-world (n=50). The primary offerings of these companies were B2B materials (n=175), B2B components (n=180), B2B equipment (n=121), B2B services (n=74), B2C products (n=64), B2C services (n=32), and Other (n=8).

2. Clayton M. Christensen, Richard Alton, Curtis Rising, and Andrew Waldeck, "The Big Idea: The New M&A Playbook," *Harvard Business Review*, March 2011. The authors describe two reasons to acquire a company: (1) to boost your company's current performance, and (2) to reinvent your business model and thereby fundamentally redirect your company. While both are problematic, the latter are "most likely to confound investors and pay off spectacularly."

3. Survey respondents self-classified themselves as individual contributors: no direct reports (n=146); middle managers: department manager, plant manager, regional manager, director (n=356); and senior leaders: C-Level, president, vice president (n=152). Because the responses were so similar between the first two classifications, "individual contributors" and "middle managers" have been grouped here as "subordinates."

4. John Morris, *Strategic Management 2E* (Corvalis, OR: Oregon State University, 2019), 35.

5. Robert S. Kaplan and David P. Norton, "The Balanced Scorecard—Measures that Drive Performance," *Harvard Business Review*, January-February 1992. The balanced scorecard measures business performance from four perspectives: customer, internal, innovation and learning, and financial.

6. David Gelles, *The Man Who Broke Capitalism: How Jack Welch Gutted the Heartland and Crushed the Soul of Corporate America—and How to Undo His Legacy* (New York: Simon and Schuster, 2022), 3.

7. Gelles, 3.

8. Gelles, 4.

9. Gelles, 59.

10. Gelles, 45-46.
11. Gelles, 65.
12. Gelles, 5.
13. Gelles, 123.
14. Gelles, 23.
15. Gelles, 45.
16. Simon Sinek, *The Infinite Game* (New York: Penguin Random House, 2019).
17. Francesco Guerrera, "Welch Condemns Share Price Focus," *Financial Times*, March 12, 2009.
18. We asked survey respondents: "How does your company's organic growth from new products and services compare?" 149 reported "weaker than competitors," 257 reported "same as competitors," and 247 reported "stronger than competitors."
19. Roger Martin, "The Age of Customer Capitalism," *Harvard Business Review*, January-February 2010.
20. Saikat Chatterjee and Thyagaraju Adinarayan, "Buy, Sell, Repeat! No Room for 'Hold' in Whipsawing Markets," *Reuters Business News*, August 3, 2020. The authors' analysis showed the average stock holding period was over seven years in the late 1950s but had steadily declined, reaching five and a half months in June 2020.
21. Simon Sinek, *Start with Why: How Great Leaders Inspire Everyone to Take Action* (New York: Penguin Random House, 2009).
22. Michael Raynor and Mumtaz Ahmed, *The Three Rules: How Exceptional Companies Think* (New York: Penguin, 2013).
23. Raynor and Ahmed, 41.
24. "List of countries by motor vehicle production," Wikipedia Foundation, last modified June 22, 2023, https://en.wikipedia.org/wiki/List_of_countries_by_motor_vehicle_production. In 1980, production numbers were: 0.48Mil (Japan) of 16.49Mil (global) in 1960; 11.04Mil (Japan) of 38.56Mil (global).
25. Dominic Barton, James Manyika, and Sarah Keohane Williamson, "The Data: Where Long-Termism Pays Off," *Harvard Business Review*, May-June 2017, 67.
26. The following assumptions were made in our financial model: The base business begins with revenue = $100 million; new product investment = 4 percent of sales (R&D + marketing); one new product is launched per $1 million of new product investment; it takes two years on average to develop a new product; each new product requires three years to reach full sales; average new product sales = $3 million; new product success rate = 40 percent; business EBITDA = 15 percent. In our high-growth model, the business doesn't simply spend more on growth; it also builds capabilities to spend it more effectively. As a result, these variables increase in the high-growth case: new product investment increases from 4 to 6 percent; average new product sales increase from $3 million to $4 million; new product success rate increases from 40 to

60 percent; incremental EBITDA from new products = 25 percent, compared to base of 15 percent. All other variables remain unchanged.

27. Louis Uchitelle, *The Disposable American: Layoffs and Their Consequences* (New York: Vintage Books, 2007).
28. Sandra J. Sucher and Marilyn Morgan Westner, "What Companies Still Get Wrong About Layoffs," *Harvard Business Review*, December 8, 2022.
29. Sandra J. Sucher and Shalene Gupta, "Layoffs That Don't Break Your Company," *Harvard Business Review*, May-June 2018.
30. Sucher and Gupta, 125.
31. Sucher and Gupta, 125.
32. Rana Foroohar, *Makers and Takers: How Wall Street Destroyed Main Street* (New York: Crown Business, 2016), x.
33. Foroohar, 6.
34. Stephen Covey, *The Seven Habits of Highly Effective People* (New York: Simon & Schuster, 1989), 54.
35. Dan Adams, *What Drives B2B Organic Growth*, 10. 540 Respondents were asked to assess twenty-four growth drivers for their impact on profitable, sustainable growth. Ten of these drivers help companies "understand" customer needs, seven help them "meet" customer needs, and seven do both. The three strongest differentiators between companies that did and did not deliver strong customer value propositions (the driver rated most important for driving growth) were all aimed at helping companies "understand" customer needs: (1) front-end work, (2) market concentration, and (3) customer interviews.
36. D.S. Hopkins and E. L. Bailey, "New Product Pressures," Conference Board Record 8, no. 6 (January 1971): 16–24. Inadequate market analysis was the leading cause of new product failures, cited by 45 percent of respondents.
37. John Benskin, John Jankowski, Audrey Kindlon, Lucien Randazzese, and J.R. Sullivan, "Understanding Unsuccessful Innovation" (working paper, NCSES 21-201, Alexandria, VA: National Science Foundation, 2021), 9. This paper looked at nineteen total case studies in nine industries, fifteen of goods, three of services, and one of new business processes. A single root cause of product failure was cited for each.
38. "The Top 12 Reasons Startups Fail," CB Insights, August 3, 2021, https://www.cbinsights.com/research/report/startup-failure-reasons-top/. This study examined the top twelve reasons for startup failure by analyzing more than 110 startup failure post-mortems.
39. Clayton M. Christensen, Taddy Hall, Karen Dillon, and David S. Duncan, "Know Your Customers' 'Jobs to Be Done,'" *Harvard Business Review*, September 2016.
40. W. Scott Burleson, *The Statue in the Stone: Decoding Customer Motivation with the 48 Laws of Jobs-to-be-Done Philosophy* (Amazon Publishing, 2020).

41. Anthony Ulwick, *What Customers Want: Using Outcome-Driven Innovation to Create Breakthrough Products and Services* (New York: McGraw-Hill, 2005).

42. Dan Adams, *What Drives B2B Organic Growth* (The AIM Institute, 2018), 10. For this survey, 540 respondents were asked to assess twenty-four growth drivers for their impact on profitable, sustainable growth. Ten of these drivers help companies "understand" customer needs, seven help them "meet" customer needs, and seven do both. The three strongest differentiators between companies that did and did not deliver strong customer value propositions (the driver rated most important for driving growth) were all aimed at helping companies "understand" customer needs: (1) front-end work, (2) market concentration, and (3) customer interviews.

43. Eric Reis, *The Lean Startup: How Today's Entrepreneurs Use Continuous Innovation to Create Radically Successful Businesses* (New York: Crown Business, 2011).

44. The Vitality Index was created by 3M in 1988 to determine a company's innovativeness through delivering new products or services. It measures new product revenues as a percent of total revenues, where *new* is typically defined as three to five years.